Up North

Up North/
Sam Cook

Illustrations by Bob Cary

Pfeifer-Hamilton

Grateful acknowledgment is made to the *Duluth News-Tribune & Herald* for permission to reprint these stories and columns, which originally appeared in that newspaper.

Pfeifer-Hamilton, Publisher
1702 E Jefferson St Duluth MN 55812 218/728-6807

Up North

Printed in the United States of America by R.R. Donnelley & Sons.
10   9   8   7   6   5   4   3   2   1

Produced by Admark Group Inc, Minneapolis MN.
Book design by Barbara Pederson, Minneapolis MN.

Library of Congress Cataloging in Publication Data
86-062906

ISBN 0-938586-09-2

The following publishers have generously given permission to use quotations from copyrighted works: From *The Singing Wilderness*, by Sigurd F. Olson, © 1956 by Sigurd F. Olson. Reprinted by permission of the publisher, Alfred A. Knopf, Inc. From *Travels with Charley*, by John Steinbeck, © 1961, 1962 by the Curtis Publishing Co., Inc.; © 1962 by John Steinbeck. Reprinted by permission of the publisher, Viking Penguin, Inc.

For Phyllis

Acknowledgments

I am indebted to many people for making this book happen. My wife, Phyllis, is not only a fine paddling partner but my best friend. Her presence is sprinkled throughout these pages. I gratefully acknowledge her support and spirit.

My parents—without really knowing it, I think—instilled in me an appreciation for the outdoors at an early age. And when it came time for me to begin exploring, they knew how to let go. I thank them for that.

So many others have been helpful and supportive. Lynnell Mickelsen offered unflagging encouragement and valuable feedback. Bob Ashenmacher, Peg Apka, Carol Copeland, Mike Furtman, Ken Gilbertson, LeAne Rutherford, David Spencer and Terry Teich helped to shape the contents of this collection. Bob Cary not only supplied his inspired illustrations, but has introduced me to many of the North Country's treasures. Don and Nancy Tubesing came to me with the idea for this book and made putting it together an enjoyable experience. I thank all of these individuals for their contributions.

I am grateful to the Duluth News-Tribune & Herald for allowing me to reprint these stories, which have appeared on its outdoor pages over the past five years.

Finally, I thank all of those friends with whom I've shared campfires and duck blinds, trout streams and ski trails. In a very real sense, this is their book as much as mine.

S.C.
Duluth, Minnesota

Contents

Up North/1

Spring

Caterpillar Nap/5
Urban Relief/8
Eve of the Opener/11
Morning/16

Summer

The Big Circle/21
The Trout Fisherman/24
Natural Wonders/31
Fast and Dirty/34
The Dream Net/36
Lucky/39
Sandwich Reflections/42

Fall

Untold Stories/49
They'd Rather Have Cash/51
Stocking Feet/58
Buck Fever/61
Death and Life/64

Winter

Dancing with a River/71
The Last Run/76
Once is Enough/82

Spring

Gearing Up/93
Back on the Brule/97
Pick of the Litter/102
Fishing Partners/105

Summer

30 Days/113
Wandering Fever/116
Words Unspoken/119
Your Fire, My Fire/122
Soul Country/127
Campfire Girl/133
Coming Home/136

Fall

Marking the Seasons/141
Forgotten Stand/144
Little Creatures/147
Brule by Night/150
Cabin Time/157
Northern Lights/160

Winter

Birkie Blues/165
A Season to Endure/170
In Stitches/173
Find the Magic/177

Up North

Up North is a certain way the wind feels on your face and the way an old wool shirt feels on your back. It's the peace that comes over you when you sit down to read one of your old trip journals, or the anticipation that bubbles inside when you start sorting through your tackle box early in the spring.

Up North is the smell of the Duluth pack hanging in your basement and the sound of pots clinking across the lake. It's a raindrop clinging to a pine needle and the dancing light of a campfire on the faces of friends.

Up North is a lone set of cross-country ski tracks across a wilderness lake and wood smoke rising from a cabin chimney. It's bunchberries in June, blueberries in July and wild rice in September.

Each of us has an Up North. It's a time and place far from the here and now. It's a map on the wall, a dream in the making, a tugging at one's soul. For those who feel the tug, who make the dream happen, who put the map in the packsack and go, the world is never quite the same again.

We have been Up North. And part of us always will be.

Spring/

Caterpillar Nap
Urban Relief
Eve of the Opener
Morning

Caterpillar Nap

I took my time looking for the spot. It had to be just right. This kind of day comes just once each spring in the North Country. I wanted to savor it. You know the kind of day—after a long winter, the first one when you can feel the sun on your back, the first day you smell the grass again, the first day you can really say it's spring. Never mind that spring came officially three weeks ago. This is the day we were looking for.

I hiked uphill, past aspen and an occasional red pine. I wanted to get over the ridge and out of the wind. It wasn't much of a breeze, but enough to make a difference on this kind of day.

Over the knoll I came to a clearing and looked around. There it was, a young jack pine surrounded by dead grass. I tossed a poncho on the ground and sat down. Perfect.

Not three feet away, a broad patch of snow and ice still held its wintry grip on the grass, but under the jack pine, out of the wind, facing the sun, it was summertime.

The poncho warmed fast in the sun. It smelled like the canvas tents we'd camped in as kids. I leaned back against the jack pine and closed my eyes. The sun baked my face, soaked into my

wool shirt, warmed my bluejeans. It was a sensation I hadn't
enjoyed since one day on a deer stand last November.

Sig Olson was right. "To anyone who has spent a winter in the
North...the first hint of spring is a major event," he wrote. "You
must live in the North to understand it."

The silence was broken by the cawing of two crows in the
distance. Somewhere thousands of feet overhead a jet murmured
across the sky. I was pondering the power and speed of the jet
when a fly landed on my leg. He seemed to be resting. I stared at
him for a moment, then reached out slowly to him. He made no
attempt to escape. Finally I touched him. Only then did he take
flight. He'll need warmer days than this one if he's to avoid
becoming another critter's meal.

Sitting in the sun felt wonderful. Lying in it felt even better.
I curled up, resting my head on my arm just inches above the
grass. The smell of those decaying grasses and moist roots
reached my nose, waking a sense that had been on sabbatical
for months.

I opened my eyes and stared into the tiny world before me.
Several layers of grass below, a tiny bug was walking down the
middle of a green shoot. I watched him for a while before I
realized I was looking right past an inch-long caterpillar. The
caterpillar was easy to miss. This wasn't one of those fuzzy
caterpillars with all the feelers. He was about the thickness of
pencil lead and the same color as the blade of dead grass he was
crawling on. Like the fly, he seemed to be waiting, gathering
strength. It was a long time before he moved, and then it was
only a short, inch-worm kind of extension.

I remember watching the caterpillar for some time, feeling the
sun on my face, my eyes beginning to close.

I don't know how long I slept. I know the caterpillar was gone
when I awoke. The sun seemed lower in the sky. The breeze
seemed cool on my neck.

I sat up and jammed my hands in my jacket pockets. I thought maybe it just seemed cooler because I'd been sleeping. I waited. The crows were still cawing in the distance. A few gulls flew over, squealing in their distinctive way. No, it wasn't the nap. The spell had passed.

I stuffed my poncho in my knapsack and headed back over the ridge, home. I followed the footprints I'd left in the snow coming in.

It had been a fleeting encounter, this brush with spring. In another month days like this would seem cool by comparison. For now, though, this was enough. We have learned, Up North, not to be greedy with spring.

Urban Relief

I'm getting itchy. What I'd like to be doing at this moment is driving down some backcountry road looking out from under the bow of my canoe. I want to park in some end-of-the-road public landing, get out, stretch, and feel the gritch of the gravel under my boots. Then I want to slip that canoe in the water, load in a couple of Duluth packs and a couple of fishing rods, and paddle off toward a cluster of islands.

I get this way every year about this time. I'm sure I'm not alone. Perhaps, if you're a steelhead angler and you spend April letting the streams rush between your legs, you don't suffer this way.

But I don't chase steelhead. And I'm getting itchy.

For some reason it seems worse this year—the waiting, the wanting. I've found myself thinking about how much city there is in me. I spend too much time on the telephone and not enough time on the back roads. I've been putting more emphasis on catching buses than I have on catching fish. I can time a string of traffic lights better than I can time a swinging shot on a ruffed grouse.

It isn't that I dislike the city, and, Lord knows, there are citier cities than Duluth. As a city dweller, I'm lucky.

I can still hear the chorus of frogs in the woods when I walk the dog at night. When I'm on my way home, the gulls are often squealing overhead. Just the other evening, I saw a pair of mallards winging low over homes and power lines. But I saw them through a bus window, and somehow the moment lacked something. I wanted to nudge the two women sitting ahead of me and say, "Look, quick—mallards. Don't you wonder where they're going? Do you suppose they're going to be nesting on Hartley Pond this spring?"

I didn't, of course. On buses you don't talk to people you don't know. The city teaches you that.

I've also been thinking back to last summer. We didn't pick blueberries—first time in a long time—and we haven't harvested wild rice for a couple of years. Sure, a lot of that had to do with the little person who came to live with us. But blueberries and wild rice are two of the things that brought us to Minnesota and made us want to stay.

Sometimes it's as easy to slip out of good patterns as it is to slip into bad ones. I don't want to let the blueberries and the wild rice get away.

What seems important about fishing and berry picking and rice harvesting is that you're out there. And when you're out there, so many other good things happen that you never predict. You see the loons dance and hear the whitethroats sing and watch the goldeneyes raise their young. You get dirt in your food and listen to noises in the night and feel small again. And that's good.

It's good because it reminds you where the real world is and what it's made of. It's water and wind and wonder, not the electrical box that glows blue and orange in the corner of your living room. It's the feel of a Duluth pack riding soft against your back, not whether you squeeze through the next intersection before the light turns red. It's the first smell of smoke from the breakfast fire, not some matrix of light bulbs beaming the time and temperature at you.

That's what counts—the little things.

If I can hold out another week or so, I'll make it. That's when we're going north.

As a 10-year-old kid on the dock of the Canadian ranger station on Saganaga Lake said one June day, "We're going to Canada." He said the word as if it were some wonderful, far-off land, a place he'd been dreaming about for years, a place he was finally going to see for himself.

I feel almost the same way.

I'm ready—ready to get some of the city out of my veins.

Eve of the Opener

A man wearing a baseball cap leans over a tank full of chub minnows. "Walleyes eat these things?" he asks.

The man who answers him wears his gray hair in a crew cut and appears to be in his mid-fifties. He leans on the other side of the chub tank, looks his customer right in the eye, and says, "The DNR has been trying to shut me down for years, these things are so deadly. You'll fill your freezer by eight in the morning."

Welcome to Pinky's Bait Shop, a memorable stop on one of Minnesota's most memorable weekends—the opening of fishing season. It's Friday night, with the season set to begin Saturday morning. Things are popping at Pinky's.

The stream of people parading through Pinky's doors has been constant since about 4 p.m. They come seeking bait—minnows, leeches, nightcrawlers—and maybe hooks or line or cigarettes or pop. But, like the man in the baseball cap, they often get a liberal dose of Pinky as well.

Pinky is Jack Jetland, 48, sole proprietor and resident character at Pinky's Bait in Grand Rapids. No one calls him Jack. To most, he's Pinky. To some, just Pink. No one is quite sure where the nickname came from.

"I guess he had red hair at one time," says a customer. That's one theory.

"Because when he was young, he had pink cheeks," says Pinky's son David, 17. Then he hedges. "Mom, that's why they call Dad Pinky, isn't it?"

"No, it's because when he was a baby, he was real pink," says Virginia Jetland, Pinky's wife.

But she, too, hedges and asks Pinky himself.

"No, it was a barber, Leo Miller, gave me that name when I was five years old," Pinky hollers across the room. "Every time I'd get in the sun, I'd get pink. He used to tease me to death."

Pinky has been in the bait business since he was a 19-year-old kid in Grand Rapids. He started out selling wholesale to bait shops and opened his own place 17 years ago. That was out on U.S. Highway 2, west of Grand Rapids in Cohasset. When the new highway bumped him out six years ago, Pinky moved into town.

You see Pinky's sign about three blocks away as you drive through Grand Rapids on Highway 2, which most anglers do on their way to lakes like Winnibigoshish, Bowstring, and Cut Foot Sioux. You see a "B" first, and an "A" right below it, in giant orange lettering on black panels. As you get closer, the "I" and "T" appear. When you can read the whole word, you'd better be ready to turn in.

Tonight the tiny parking lot looks like a homecoming parade that ran amok. Cars and boats, trucks and boats, and campers and boats are parked every which way. People spill out, hitch up their pants, and sidle through Pinky's propped-open screen door —or try to.

"Oh, God," says a middle-aged woman, stopping short at the door. She is overwhelmed at the number of people milling about the small shop. This is Pinky's on opening weekend.

If you can get inside, you find Pinky's is a lot like other bait shops—bubbling tanks of minnows, coolers full of leeches and nightcrawlers, landing nets and anchors, pegboards full of tackle and car-top boat carriers and sunglasses and candy bars and caps.

A few things tell you this place might be different. Those bumper stickers, for one:

"Dump the DNR"

"Ration government, not gasoline".

"Don't reelect anybody"

And you can't help but notice those personal checks, presumably the bouncing variety, taped to a big piece of cardboard behind the counter. "I used to have 'em under the word 'deadbeats,'" Pinky says. "They told me to take 'deadbeats' down. I could have gotten in trouble for defamation of character."

Other things make Pinky's different, too, but they aren't so readily apparent. You have to pick them up from someone like Gary Sorenson, a Grand Rapids guide who has stopped in for minnows.

"One thing about Pinky is he always gives you a good count," Sorenson says. "His tanks are clean and fresh. And there's good variety. That's so important.

"In the summer when I'm fishing for 10- and 15-pound northerns, we're using 10- or 12-inch sucker minnows, and this is the only place you can get 'em. Pinky makes a special trip just to get 'em. If he tells you he'll have 'em in a couple days, you come in in a couple days and you got 'em.

"The information he gives you on lakes is reliable. He's one of the very few that I'll tell where they're hitting, because I know the next time I come in, if I need to know, he'll tell me straight."

Tonight Sorenson isn't seeking that kind of advice. He just needs a couple of dozen minnows. But he hangs around. "It's just fun to come in to watch the madness," he says.

Through the weekend, Pinky's will move something like 250 gallons of minnows. A gallon of minnows contains from 50 to 150 dozen minnows, depending on their size, Pinky says. At an average of 100 dozen per gallon, that's 300,000 minnows for opening weekend.

Pinky's will also move 30 or 40 gallons of leeches this weekend. That's 30 or 40 gallons of leeches sorted into small, medium, large and jumbo sizes.

And nightcrawlers? "You wouldn't believe it," says Virginia. "You gotta pick 'em off the floor in the back room. They're overflowing the coolers. We probably have 10,000."

Like the four Jetland children, who range in age from 9 to 18, Virginia is putting in long hours this weekend. At the moment, she is sorting leeches from a bucket into plastic containers atop a gas stove in the corner of the shop. She complains that the leeches smell, but she confesses to having a good time on opening weekend.

"It's kind of exciting," she says. "You think about it in the winter and kind of dread it. But you get into it, and it's fun."

Daughter Jackie, 18, sits on a stool across the room selling fishing licenses. David has just returned from Winnibigoshish Lake with a truckload of shiner minnows. Kenny, 14, "is probably in the house eating," Virginia says. "He loves to eat." Kevin, 9, is walking around stocking-footed on the damp floor, wondering if he can go fishing tomorrow.

The parade continues.
"Are these things guaranteed to catch fish?"
"Where can a guy get a hamburger around here?"
"How long will these things keep?"
"You gonna stay open all night?"

Pinky used to stay open all night before opening day. That's not the plan this year. He'll close at about 1 a.m. and reopen about 4 a.m. But if he thought it would make enough difference, he'd stay open. He's not afraid of work.

"I've always said if I couldn't make it working 10 hours a day, I'd work 12. If I couldn't make it working 12, I'd work 14. Most guys won't do that," he says.

He is talking about the bait business, but one detects his personal philosophy slipping in. He loves a good ear, and he gets cranked up easily. The Department of Natural Resources is one of his favorite targets.

"Right here," he says, grabbing one of his DNR bumper stickers. "I'll pump this stuff. The DNR is derelict in its duties. Fishing has declined steadily, and they do nothing about it. Instead, they build a two-and-a-half-million-dollar office building.

"I got no complaints against the guy sittin' in the truck. It's the bureaucracy. It's the legislature that gives 'em two and a half million dollars for a new office building. This is my office." He points through a doorway under a mounted northern pike with a Reese's Peanut Butter Cup in its jaws, to a cubbyhole with a desk in the corner. "And if I made $5,000 more this year, I wouldn't put it into my office.

"I gotta go out and get cold and wet and miserable to get bait. How do they figure they can raise fish without getting cold and wet and miserable?"

While he is saying these things, Virginia is looking up at him from her leech sorting. She's scowling.

"I don't want to get in a bind, but that's my beliefs," Pinky explains. "I'm overbearing as hell, and I get myself in a lot of trouble."

But not with his customers. They love him. A man with three young children pauses at the screen door on his way out, and turns to the children. "Say good-bye to Pinky," he tells them.

"Goodbye," they chime.

Pinky smiles.

"One thing about the fishing clientele," he says. "It's the greatest in the world. They're always happy."

Especially on opening weekend. Especially at Pinky's.

Morning

Morning had broken on the small lake. Mist was hanging over the water in lazy ghosts. The ghosts thickened in the distance, obscuring the far shoreline. It was spring in the canoe country.

We had come for rainbow trout, and we had already found a few. But as it almost always is in the wilderness, we had found more than we expected. This morning was such a find.

I can still see it in my mind as if I were there. Bob Cary was coaxing the breakfast fire to life. The blackened coffee pot, filled with lake water, sat atop the grate. Only the two of us were up, the others still sleeping in the tents.

We went about our little chores quietly, speaking in hushed tones when speech was necessary. Occasionally we'd catch each other simply standing, staring out over the lake.

The sun had risen now, though we couldn't see it. Its presence gave the mist a peach glow unlike anything I'd ever seen before.

The coffee was almost to a boil when we heard the sound. It started as a low cry, somewhere beyond the ridge behind us. Instinctively, we froze. Then the sound began to grow, like a noon whistle in some farm town. Soon it was joined by others, until it became a wild, wailing chorus. Wolves.

For 30 seconds, their cries filled the morning air. I tried to imagine how many were in the pack and what had prompted them to sing at this moment. No sooner had I begun to reason, it seemed, than they stopped.

No longer was the morning the same. It had been beautiful. It had been spellbinding. Now it was beyond that.

The memory is lodged somewhere in the recesses of my mind. It's back there with the sandhill cranes that flew over the Gods River one evening as the sun was setting. It's there with the groaning of ice under the snow house where we spent New Year's Eve.

All of them are there, with a hundred more. Sometimes, when I'm staring deep into a fire or gazing at the northern lights, the images and the sounds come back. And I know I am a rich man.

Summer/

The Big Circle
The Trout Fisherman
Natural Wonders
Fast and Dirty
The Dream Net
Lucky
Sandwich Reflections

The Big Circle

We met the two men on one of the portages leading to Knife Lake. We were on our way into the woods for a week. They were on their way home.

What I remember best is the cooler those two men were carrying. They opened it and showed us the fish they'd caught in Knife, the biggest lake trout I'd ever seen.

My wife and I were making our first trip together into the border country. We were green to the ways of the woods then and, to be honest, a little apprehensive.

It was reassuring to meet a couple of woodsmen who seemed so comfortable, so at home. They were from Duluth, they said. They came up to Knife as many weekends as they could, always to fish lake trout. They were portaging a square-stern canoe and motor.

"We can leave Duluth and be on Knife in six hours," one of them said.

After we'd chatted for a while, I got up enough nerve to ask the men a favor. Phyllis and I had been outfitted for our trip by an Ely outfitter. We'd stopped at lunch to look through our packs to see if we had everything we needed. We had found no rope. We would need some if we were going to hang our food pack and keep it away from the bears.

I told the men our problem and asked them if they had some rope they could spare. They didn't hesitate. One of them dug into a worn Duluth pack and pulled out two hunks of rope.

I was a little embarrassed asking for the rope. It wasn't like we were just borrowing it. I knew we'd never see the men again. They knew it too. But they gladly gave us all we needed.

We chatted a little more, then went our opposite ways down the portage.

I guess that was one of the first times I found myself a part of the Big Circle. Back then I had no conception what the Big Circle was. In fact, I'd never heard it called that until a few summers ago, when a bush pilot at an Indian village in northern Manitoba referred to it. The pilot had opened his home to us that afternoon, prepared us lunch, and let us take a shower. We'd tried to thank him and asked how we could repay him.

"Forget it," he said. "You'll do someone else a favor sometime. It's all part of the Big Circle."

I liked the concept. Because of the nature of bush travel, you often can't repay those who help you. But you can help somebody else, somewhere down the trail.

Sooner or later, it all comes around again. That's the Big Circle.

Phyllis and I have never again seen those two men who gave us the rope that day on the portage. But a few years later, deep in Ontario's Quetico Provincial Park, we showed a couple from Colorado some good spots to camp and fish. It was their first trip to the canoe country, and they appreciated the information.

I never realized I was part of the Big Circle when John Stone and Don Wenger from my hometown in Kansas took a group of us north on a nine-day canoe trip 20 years ago. I don't suppose I ever fully appreciated what those men had done until recently, when I accompanied a bunch of Minnesota Scouts on a 300-mile bicycle trip.

I didn't think anything of it when three of us opened our campsite to a couple of weary women on the Kekekabic Trail one September, either. But then, there I was the next summer in a remote Manitoba Indian village, eating lunch served by a bush pilot I'd met just a few hours before.

That's the way the Big Circle works. You never know when you're going to find yourself in a position where you need a hand. You never know when you'll have the next chance to offer yours.

One summer Mike Furtman and I stopped at a restaurant in Two Harbors for breakfast on our way up to do some fishing in the Boundary Waters Canoe Area Wilderness. Furtman had just written a book called *A Boundary Waters Fishing Guide.*

The couple in the next booth were dressed as if they, too, were headed for the woods. The man leaned over our booth and said, "Excuse me, but do you guys know anything about fishing in the Boundary Waters?"

Furtman and I looked at each other, then smiled. We spent the next several minutes recommending a lake, drawing a map of it on a napkin, and talking about how to catch smallmouth bass.

We felt good. Probably about as good as a couple of Duluth men felt 10 years ago when they gave those greenhorn paddlers the rope they needed.

The Trout Fisherman

At first it had looked like a trail, not a worn path, but a meandering opening among the thimbleberries. The trail dissolved into the forest, but that didn't bother Enok Olson. Now he was coursing randomly through the aspen and large-leafed aster, stepping over deadfalls, and batting branches away from his face.

It didn't seem that he was trying to find the stream so much as he was being drawn to it. Perhaps that's the way it is when you're almost 89, and brook trout streams have been drawing you to their banks for half a century.

Olson pulled up and leaned against an aspen. His entourage —Lloyd Gilbertson and myself—found our own leaning trees and caught our breath.

"This is tough," Olson said.

It was tough, tougher than the brook trout fishing Olson does closer to his cabin home near Silver Bay, Minnesota. There a neighbor woman drops him off at a bridge on a nearby river and returns to pick him up later in the day.

We were a few miles up the Gunflint Trail north of Grand Marais, crashing through the brush, seeking a stream Olson hadn't fished since he was, oh, probably 83.

The stream has a name, of course, but it won't be used here. "It would be better if you didn't mention it," Olson had said. It isn't that he wants to keep the fishing for himself. He will likely never set a hip boot in this stream again after this visit. But Olson is a trout fisherman. It's the principle of the thing.

Soon we were wandering again, Olson out in front with his fly rod in one hand and his walking stick in the other. He moved along steadily, past the rose hips and alders and balsams.

Watching Olson up ahead was like seeing the cover of a 1920 L.L. Bean catalog come to life. He wore an old gray fishing cap and an ancient fishing coat whose corduroy collar was frayed from years of rubbing against a whiskered neck. The coat, of heavy cotton duck, was originally a tawny brown, but the years and the North Shore weather have mellowed it to a gentle buff.

Olson's khaki pants disappeared at knee level into his turned-down hip boots. The boots, too, showed the years. Patches were covered with more patches, and the felt that Olson glued on the soles of the boots was all but gone.

His walking stick was an alder, waist-high and stout. His fiberglass fly rod bore the scars of many treks like this one. Its varnish was scratched, and a couple of its guides were bent.

It was the creel, more than anything else, that gave Olson's outfit its character. A classic creel like Olson's is a wicker basket that trout anglers put their fish in. Olson's hung from one shoulder and rested against his hip as if it were part of him. "It's 40 years old," he said. "I used to get these from Michigan Willow for $3 or $4. Now I couldn't buy one for $50." The bottom of the creel had long since broken out—the victim of too many riverside slips and falls. Olson had patched it with the tin of some old coffee cans. The tin is held in place by pieces of wire woven through the remaining wicker.

On we went. The terrain began to drop, though the stream was nowhere in sight. Soon the descent was so steep we had to walk sideways to maintain our footing. Olson clutched at branches and grabbed onto birch trunks, using his arms to help his legs.

"I just wish I was about 20 years younger," he said.

Olson's companions let the remark sink in. One couldn't help but wonder when even a 69-year-old had last clambered down this hill.

Soon we could hear the stream, and finally, after sliding part way on our rear ends and climbing through some cedars, we were there.

At one of our pauses on the way down, Olson had said, "We may not get any fish, but I know you're gonna marvel when you see that river." He was right. This wasn't just a stream. It was a canyon. Sheer walls of sedimentary rock rose from the water's edge, some 40 feet high. Where there were no walls, the valley rose at a pitch like the one we had just slid down.

The water was low, almost as low as Olson ever remembered seeing it. In the shallows it was the color of weak tea, but coffee brown in the pools below ledges and along those sheer walls.

Olson couldn't wait to get a worm on his hook and get it in the water. He wasn't asking for much. "If I get one fish, I'm happy," he said. "If I get two fish, I'm really happy."

He pulled his hip boots up, put his walking stick in front of him, and waded into the stream. It's hard to imagine what it must be like to be stream fishing at 89, when your eyes won't see all you want them to see and your wading legs aren't as steady as they once were.

"I can't see the hook, so I gotta go by feel when I put a worm on," Olson said.

His feel is good. He had a worm on in no time and flipped it into a pool of fast water below a ledge.

"There could be a fish in here, but I don't think so," Olson said.

With his walking stick clamped under one arm, he played out line. Suddenly, he raised his rod tip, the line tightened, and a fish was dancing on the surface of the pool.

"He's got one!" Gilbertson hollered.

He had one, all right. Olson dropped his walking stick and began working line in. A broad grin spread across his face. He had made it back to his river. He had caught a fish. He was a happy man.

But he hadn't landed his fish yet. He picked up his walking stick, and keeping his line tight, shuffled over to the far shore. He tossed his walking stick behind him and reached inside his fishing coat. From an inside pocket, he pulled out a landing net, the collapsible kind, with a rim of flexible metal that sprung into a full hoop when it was released.

Olson popped the net open, stooped over the water, and pulled his fish close. It was a small brook trout, but nice by inland stream standards. Olson drew it along the surface until it was over the landing net. Then he scooped the brookie up and rose to his feet, beaming.

Hands shaking ever so slightly, he felt for the hook, found it, and pulled it free. Holding onto the fish with his whole hand, he slipped it into the creel.

As Olson refolded the net and stuck it back in his jacket, Gilbertson, 35, asked him a question. "How many trout have you caught now Enok?"

Olson thought for a moment. "Well, this year, I'm probably in the 50s," he said.

"No, I mean always," Gilbertson said.

"Oh, for heaven's sake," Olson said.

Olson, one of nine children, was born in southern Sweden in 1895. He and his wife of 61 years, Esther, came to the United States as newlyweds in 1923. They could speak no English, but it wasn't long before Enok, an electrician, hooked up with Minnesota Power, where he worked for the next 37 years.

During those years Enok and Esther went to the woods as often as they could.

"Esther would have all of our things ready on Friday evening," Enok said. "If I'd get home at 5:30, we'd be ready to go by 6:00."

They fished almost all of the North Shore streams, crashing into the backcountry and making camps in the middle of nowhere. Their love of the North Shore led them to build a modest cabin three miles east of Silver Bay. They retired there in 1960, and live there still on what is now called the Olson Road.

Someone asked Enok whether the road was named after him.

"It's like this," he said. "There's the Lincoln Monument, the Washington Memorial, and the Olson Road. All important people have something named after them."

Enok's days usually start about 4 a.m., when he and Esther wake up. A typical breakfast is the one he had before this week's fishing trip—fried potatoes, pickled herring, a hard-boiled egg, and coffee.

He loves to work with wood in his shop. He makes oversized wooden cribbage boards "for the old people."

Spend a day on the river with Enok, and you will come to know a gentle, yet spunky man. You'll hear about the deer he shot on opening day of deer season in 1941, the day he became a U.S. citizen, his first day on the job in America. And you'll hear fishing stories. Many involve his brother—or "brudder" as Enok pronounces it—who was also quite a trout fisherman.

"I found this stream, and it was a good one," he said. "I'd been fishing it for quite a while, and I always caught fish. I never told my brudder about it. Finally, I told him , 'OK, I'll take you there.' So one day I take him. We get in there and he says, 'Oh, I been fishing this spot for a long time.'"

Enok isn't given to exaggeration, even when it comes to fishing. "I wouldn't lie a half inch about the size of a trout," he said. "But if someone asks me, 'Where'd you get all those nice trout?' I'll lie like an SOB."

If you spend that day with Enok, you will also come to understand a little about being old. Enok knows. He's had more experience at it than most people.

"Don't think it isn't miserable being old," he will say. He became a member of the North Shore Golden Age Club in Silver

Bay. He liked the club, but wanted to change its name. "I wanted to call it the North Shore Senior Citizens Club," he said. "It isn't the Golden Age. The first year after you retire, it's the Golden Age. After that, it gets tough."

It was midday on the river. Olson had worked upstream from the pool where he caught his first fish, looking for a hole he remembered. He would sit there, he said.

Gilbertson and I fished downstream. We caught and kept about 10 trout, releasing many more. None were big—10 inches tops—but they were electric with fight. Then we headed back to find our partner.

We came around one of the river's precipitous bends, and there he was. He had found his hole. He was sitting on a cedar log that hung over a ledge. The stream ran wide and shallow over the ledge, then dropped three or four feet into one of the finest looking holes a trout fisherman would ever want to see.

Olson was literally part of the river. As he sat there, the water flowed under and on both sides of him. Both his feet were in the water. His worm was in the pool.

We walked on up to see him.

"I've got three fish," he said. "Did you catch anything?"

We told him we'd caught brookies, rainbows, and one brown. He seemed even happier about our luck than he was about the three brookies lying on damp cedar boughs in that patched creel of his. And remember, one would have made him happy.

While Gilbertson cooked trout on a stick over a tiny fire, Olson talked. His blue eyes danced like the river before him as he told us of bygone fishing trips. We ate fish and licked fingers and listened to the river.

The climb out of the canyon was a workout. Nine times we stopped to rest.

"The doc says my ticker's good, so I don't worry about that," Olson said.

That was good to hear. He was probably the only one among us who wasn't worried about that ticker.

On we climbed.

"I think this hill's steeper than it used to be," Olson said.

We stopped to rest again.

"I won't say it yet, but when we get to the top, I'll say it was a damn nice trip," Olson said.

Up we went—and up. Occasionally, Olson would grab a birch tree and Gilbertson—6-foot-5 and 230 pounds—would give him a shove. But almost every step out of that valley was Olson's own. It was simply a matter of time.

Finally we reached the top of the ridge and followed a trail to a pasture. From there it was a quarter-mile walk to our car. Because the sun was hot, we took it slowly.

When we turned down a lane and saw the car, Olson spoke. "Is it all right to say I made it now?"

"You made it, Enok," Gilbertson said.

"Well, I wasn't too damn sure I would either."

Olson had returned to his river. He had found his way in there, caught some fish and made the climb out.

A fellow couldn't help recalling something Olson had said, sitting there by the stream eating lunch. The water was cascading into that pool and three trout were lying in Olson's creel and the smoke from the fire smelled like every fire ever built beside a stream. "I'm glad I had a chance to fish this one more time," he had said. "It's beautiful."

He knew—he had to know—that he wouldn't be coming back again, not to the canyon. But he had shared his river with a couple of youngsters who knew what it meant to him. They will go back, and when they do, Olson will always be with them.

Natural Wonders

Supper was cooking over a small fire when we heard the cry. We weren't in the kind of place where you'd expect to hear such a scream. We were camped on Suzanette Lake in Ontario's Quetico Provincial Park in early September. In five days we had seen only one other canoe party. The sounds we were accustomed to hearing were wind in the pines and waves on the rocks.

The cry came again, quickly, a half-human, half-animal wail. We looked at one another, then ran to the water's edge to see what was happening. We might have guessed it would be a loon, but this loon had a problem. He passed over our point at tree-top level, flying fast. About 10 yards behind him, and definitely in pursuit, was a mature bald eagle. They went over as if they were flying in formation.

The loon sailed down onto the water, made a rather ungraceful landing and, in almost the same motion, dived under. The eagle swooped down over the roil of water where the loon had disappeared, then coasted up to a pine bough on the opposite shore of our bay.

In a moment the loon surfaced, then immediately dived again. The eagle didn't move.

We aren't sure how long this little game went on before the eagle gave up. We went back to camp and finished preparing supper.

We couldn't help wondering why the eagle was chasing the loon. A matter of territory? Competition over a fish supper? Or maybe an eagle who just liked the sound of a loon dinner?

The questions will go unanswered. What is meaningful, it seems, is that the encounter took place, and that we were lucky enough to witness it.

When we head for the backcountry, all of us hope to see some wildlife—moose, beaver, or if we're very lucky, maybe an otter or mink. Sometimes, though, we get more than we bargain for. We steal a glimpse of interaction between the critters who call the wild places home.

It happened twice again on the same 10-day trip. Two days before, we had caught a two-pound smallmouth bass in the Darky River. In its stomach was the partially digested but unmistakable body of a mouse. Had the mouse been swimming where it shouldn't have been? Had it fallen in the water from some overhanging branch? We'll never know.

Later in the trip, we paddled around a small island just off the mainland in Kahshahpiwi Lake. The quick movement of a brown form on the mainland caught our eyes. It was an otter chasing a squirrel. The squirrel scampered up a tree. Foiled, the otter headed for the water. He plunked in, went under, and came up halfway to the island with a small fish in his mouth. Climbing onto some rocks on the island's shore, the otter ate the fish and scurried off.

An otter eating a fish? Yes. But chasing a squirrel? Why? For fun? For food? We'll never know.

But that's all right. Our world is full of the predictable and patterned. We need a good dose of wonder once in a while, happenings that make us just shake our heads and rub our chins. But chances are, we won't find those things in the city park or at the scenic overlook. We have to get back in the boonies. We have to tromp around and get bitten by bugs and get smoke in our eyes and water in our boots.

If we're lucky, we'll come away with more questions than answers.

Fast and Dirty

One of the best things about picking blueberries is that it puts an ample supply of the succulent little berries into the freezer. That, subsequently, results in a lot of good eating for the next few weeks, months, or year, depending upon how productive you are as a picker.

But having blueberries on hand is just one benefit of picking blueberries. There's another by-product of the annual endeavor some folks are apt to overlook: you can tell a lot about a person by the way he or she goes about the task of picking.

Send 10 people out to the nearest cutover to pick and check their results a couple of hours later. You'll find that most people fall into one of two general picking categories: the fast-and-dirty or the slow-and-clean.

Fast-and-dirty folks can fill their pails up lickety-split. Never mind if there are a few leaves and twigs and bugs and dirt in with the berries. Just get 'em in the bucket. There'll be time to clean 'em later.

Then there's the slow-and-clean crowd. Neatness counts with these folks. The pail of a slow-and-clean picker may not fill up fast, but when it's full, it's full of ready-to-eat berries. No leaves, no sticks, just blueberries on top of blueberries. Trying to change a slow-and-clean to a fast-and-dirty, or vice versa, is like asking someone to change religions. It doesn't go over very big.

That is why I believe in premarital picking. In fact, I think it ought to be required of all couples who are engaged. Sure, they may think they're in love, but get 'em out in that blueberry patch for a few hours and they'll find out for sure.

You see, a person's picking habits say a lot about what kind of mate he or she is going to be.

A fast-and-dirty picker is the kind of person who is almost sure to squeeze the toothpaste tube in the middle, leave the empty cardboard cylinder on the toilet paper dispenser instead of getting a new roll out, and sleep across the centerline of the bed.

The slow-and-clean freaks, of course, always have exactly the same number of hangers in the closet as there are items to hang, never wear a pair of underwear they would be embarrassed to be seen in during a medical emergency, and spend most of their free time straightening pictures on the livingroom wall.

You can see how important it is, then, that people who plan to be together until death do they part spend a little time together berry picking.

Now, this isn't to say that a slow-and-clean and a fast-and-dirty are totally incompatible. In fact, that may not be the case at all. They say opposites attract, don't they?

Can you imagine what the bathroom of two fast-and-dirties would look like? Or can you see the hanger battles that could result from two slow-and-cleans living together?

Perhaps it would all work out. I don't know. The point is, these people should at least have an idea of what they're getting into before they tie the knot. I think it might make for a lot more long, happy marriages. Or, to put it another way, the couple who picks together sticks together.

The Dream Net

She is sleeping now. Morning light filters through the window and bathes the cradle where she lies. Over her head, suspended on fine thread, hangs the dream net. It's a simple creation, a five-inch band of wood with a web of linen stretching across it. In the middle of the web, there's a small hole. Through the hole, according to Chippewa folklore, good dreams pass through to the sleeping child. The bad dreams get tangled in the net, and when the light strikes them in the morning, they die.

The net must have been working this summer morning. The infant slept peacefully. Her tiny eyebrows rose occasionally, and little squeaks came out of her mouth now and then. It was impossible to know what was going through that six-day-old mind of hers, but the thoughts must have been pleasant.

The dream net guarding her sleep was made by Audrey Wyman, a 60-year-old Wrenshall woman who loves the natural world. Though not an Indian herself, Wyman grew up near the Lac Courte Oreilles band of Chippewa outside of Hayward, Wisconsin. There she learned to speak the Ojibway language and came to know some of the Chippewa customs.

Wyman doesn't know the little girl who sleeps under the dream net, but she knew of the little girl's father, and something of his dreams. Wyman knew he was full of wonder about this new person coming into his life, and how her dreams would mesh with his. So the woman had passed on the dream net with a little advice. "Don't worry. You can still pursue your dreams. I have 14 children of my own. I know."

She had made the dream net's circular frame from a black ash tree. "You have to get it in the spring, when the sap is up," she said.

She described the process, beginning with the part about sprinkling some tobacco on the ground near the tree she had selected.

"When Ojibway people take a plant for use from the woods, they talk to the plant," she said. "In a way, it's like a prayer or an affirmation that the plant will be used for a good purpose. It's sort of explaining why you need it.

"Traditionally, you put a pinch of tobacco on the ground beside the plant before you take it. That's quite important, especially with a plant where you have to destroy it before you use it."

Then she had peeled and soaked the log until she could strip away the thin piece of wood she needed. She formed it into a circle, then began weaving the web of linen inside of it.

"It's something I figured out myself," she said. "Traditionally, I think the Indians used the same knot that's used in a fisherman's net. I didn't know how to do that. I just start at the outside and tie a little overhand knot in each loop. It comes out in a spiral design.

"That isn't the only way to make a dream net," she said. "People make them many different ways. Some decorate them a whole lot. Some are plain. Some bands make them without any hole in the center. Their idea is it only catches the bad dreams.

"The other idea is that the good dreams get through. They're round and perfect, so they go through the hole. I think the hole's important . One of the problems with the modern world is that we work so hard to get rid of the bad dreams, we lose the good ones too."

Wyman has made several dream nets, she said. She made some for her younger children, others for her grandchildren.

"I have one for myself that's 14 inches across," she said. "I have big dreams." She laughed. "I made it from the outer hoop of an old hickory packbasket that I carried for miles and miles until it went to dust."

The little girl's father pondered Wyman's remarks as he watched his daughter sleeping beneath the dream net. Already he finds himself wondering less about his own dreams and more about hers.

Lucky

He knows he's lucky, the fellow paddling stern, lucky because of the woman paddling bow. Lord knows, he's had plenty of time to think about it, looking at her back all those miles they've paddled together. He's looked at her so long he can see her with his eyes shut—the old, green plaid shirt she always wears camping, the green felt hat with the hole chewed out of it by a squirrel, her wiry little arms swinging the black plastic paddle as if it were part of her.

"Switch," he says.

They swing their paddles to the opposite sides and continue down the lake.

He thinks of all the times he's talked to someone about the wilderness he loves, and responded to the inevitable question, "Your wife—does she like to get out, too?"

He always answers without thinking. Of course, she does. He never questioned that. What if she didn't? What if he always had to leave her when he went to the woods? Would he go nearly as often as he does now? What would it be like? He can't imagine.

He wonders what she thinks about while he's thinking about her as they paddle. He wonders, when she paddles stern, if she looks at him as much as he looks at her.

She's so small—a shade over five feet, maybe 110 pounds, but tough. She can swing that paddle all day into the wind. She carries the food pack both early and late in the trip.

"Switch."

It's more than her physical strength. She can handle the bugs. She can take the rain. She can laugh when she's up to her knees in the muck of a portage. That's worth a lot in the bush.

He remembers their first trip together into the backcountry. It had been raining, and they couldn't get a fire going. They had eaten peanut butter and jelly sandwiches for breakfast and laughed about it later.

It hasn't always been smiles. He remembers the time on a portage when she dropped the pack with the camera equipment. Frustrated, he shouted at her, something about being more careful. Then he looked up and saw the other couple waiting to get past. Thinking back on it, he feels embarrassed. She still gets a kick out of that one.

"Switch."

Somewhere along the way, she started going into the woods on her own—not by herself, with other women. They looked up to her as a leader. It changed the whole way he felt about her in the woods. She seemed like an equal after that, as if he were out with one of his fishing buddies. It didn't matter who built the fire, who split the wood, who cleaned the fish, or who strung up the rope for the food pack.

Looking back, he's sure that she always could have done those things on trips with him, but for some reason, he had felt he had to take care of her. He had to do certain tasks. He had felt responsible.

"Switch."

He knows, now, who did the most learning when she was out on those other trips. He wonders, if she hadn't made the trips, if he ever would have caught on. He's afraid he knows the answer. No matter. They're beyond that now.

It feels good, paddling with her. He watches her strokes, times his with hers. The canoe moves along steadily. Lucky man, that stern paddler.

Sandwich Reflections

Lunch was a turkey sandwich and a Pepsi. I was sitting outside at one of those umbrella tables that blossom in downtown Duluth when summer arrives for real. Not 50 yards away, a massive John Deere track-mounted claw was plucking up huge chunks of Superior Street. The machine would curl its appendage, lift its load in uneven monster jerks, then open its maw and let the former street clunk into a waiting truck bed. Dust rose from the truck, and the claw's diesel engine revved for another mouthful of asphalt.

My mind wandered. I recalled some of the other places I've had lunch. I remembered, in particular, a lunch I had a couple of summers ago. Eight of us were on a limestone riverbank about 80 miles from Hudson Bay in northern Manitoba. The canoes were pulled nose up on shore. It was August, but cold. In the pictures we're wearing wool shirts and stocking caps.

We had been on the trail for most of three weeks. A few days before, we had run out of jelly. That left the Ry-Krisp crackers and the peanut butter. Still, it was a good lunch — not as good as when we'd had the jelly, but good just the same.

It was good because we were in new country and because we were exploring. And we weren't just exploring a river. We were exploring our own limits—our fears, our judgment, our physical capabilities. The river just happened to be going the same way.

The trip was big—three weeks on the water, a month away from home, hundreds of miles from the last outpost of what we call civilization. In those three weeks, we had run bigger rapids than most of us had seen before, made longer portages than most of us had made before, paddled more miles in a day, seen more mosquitoes, and carried heavier packs.

I remember looking forward to that trip, wondering what it would be like as I pondered that little blue line on the map that wiggled all the way to Hudson Bay. Trips like that have a way of taking on a larger-than-life quality, until one morning, you toss your gear in a van, load up the canoes and do it. Then it all seems so natural. The drama unfolds moment by moment, rapid by rapid, campsite by campsite. You do what must be done, because no one else is going to do it for you. Difficulties are surmounted. Challenges are met.

Then—always too soon—it's over. You're back in the concrete and clutter, wearing clean clothes and trying to smell good and watching some steel claw go about remodeling the chunk of civilization you call home.

I took a sip of the Pepsi and wished it were river water. Sitting there, thinking back to that lunch on the limestone river bank and the rest of that trip, I was surprised at what we'd done. Already some of those rapids seemed more formidable in my mind than they had when we were riding them. The portages seemed longer. The mosquitoes seemed thicker. Not in a bragging, "look-what-we-did" way, but in a personal, reflective sense, it all seemed bigger now than it had seemed when we were there.

I think that's the way it is when, as youngsters, we listen to tales from deer camp, or when, as adults, we hear someone tell about salmon fishing in Alaska or paddling to Hudson Bay. We tend to put those experiences in the dream category for so long before we make them happen that when we do finally make them come true, they seem relatively simple. Sometimes we even feel a sense of disappointment that the dream has been fulfilled. Then we must find new dreams to replace the old.

Along the way, we grow. We push ourselves and teach ourselves and surprise ourselves. We reach out and risk and sometimes fail. But always, if we're exploring, we're growing. Ultimately, we have a rich reservoir of memories that is sweet to draw upon when life seems mundane and ordinary, when life is another turkey sandwich and another Pepsi, and a giant claw is making dust where a street used to be.

Fall/

Untold Stories
They'd Rather Have Cash
Stocking Feet
Buck Fever
Death and Life

Untold Stories

Sometimes, just for a minute, I wish I didn't hunt, because I would like to see what this business of hunting looks like to a nonhunter.

And sometime I'm going to take a nonhunter hunting for a day, so he or she can see what hunting looks like from my point of view. Not so the two of us can walk off into the sunset hand-in-hand, but simply so we can understand each other a little better. I think we have a lot more in common than we might realize.

Part of the reason for the gap between us now is the way we hunters paint the picture of our outings. Our talk is almost always of the way we dropped the big buck, the day we doubled on pheasants or the time we killed two ducks with one shot. These are the success stories, the ones that are fun to tell. They represent only a tiny fraction of the time we spend in the field. But to the nonhunter, the casual listener at the office coffee break or the friend's wife at the dinner party, it must seem as if we spend most of our time in the woods blasting away with shotguns and rifles.

Hunters don't often talk about the countless hours we spent sitting on a deer stand up in some popple tree, listening to the November forest. We rarely describe that quiet moment in the duck blind when the marsh hawk flew by 20 feet away. We don't talk about the sunny October grouse hunt when we sat down, laid our shotgun across our lap, and stole one of those wonderfully warm naps.

When we do talk about those things, we usually are talking to our fellow hunters. Why? Because we know they'll understand. We know they'll care. We know they've been there.

Something else is at work here, too—time. When we share those quiet moments, those memorable morsels that make our hunts so rich, we often do it while we're hunting, or maybe back at the deer shack, where we have the leisure to dissect our hunts.

Back at the office, or at the party, we must condense and edit. What does your secretary or the guy at the next desk ask when you return from your deer hunt? Nine out of ten times, it's "Well, did you get your buck?" When you get back from your Manitoba duck hunt, they ask, "Well, did you have good shooting?"

We give them just what they want. If we got the buck, they get the 20-second, standing-at-the-coffee-machine account of the kill. If we didn't, we give them the 10-second answer, "No, but our party did real well," and we trot back to our work station.

Just once, I'd like to say, "No, but let me tell you about the morning the pine marten ran past my deer stand." Or, "Yes, we shot a lot of ducks, but if I were allowed only one memory, it would be the one where we were paddling across the lake in the dark, with the stars reflecting in the water, when we heard the wing beats of unseen ducks above us. If you have a minute, I'd like to tell you about it."

It is experiences like those, along with the million moments of uneventful waiting that string them together, that color hunts. To most hunters, those moments are just as significant as the chance to do some shooting. It's too bad that few outside our own little fraternity ever hear about them.

They'd Rather Have Cash

Curtis Johnson laid his three fox pelts on the table without saying a word. He jammed his hands into his jeans pockets and waited.

L.L. "Newt" Newton, an inch of ashes somehow clinging to the end of his cigar, stretched each skin to its full length. He picked up a brush and began stroking the hides. With the experience that has come from buying furs for most of his 80 years, Newton scrutinized the pelts before him.

"Couldn't get any males, eh?" Newton asked from behind his bobbing cigar.

"Nope," Johnson said.

Newton ran a hand over one hide. Then he slipped two fingers of the same hand up next to his lips, squeezed the cigar, and took it out of his mouth.

"Forty each on the big ones," he called across the room to Steve Picht. "Thirty on the small one."

Johnson, 20, couldn't keep the smile off his face. "Fair enough," he said. "Fair enough."

North America's centuries-old fur trade had come to life again at its most basic level: the transaction completed over and over each day at Newton Furs in Grand Rapids, Minnesota.

The place is a legend in these parts, mainly because Newton is a legend himself.

"He's a hell of a great guy," said Deer River's Tom Stuber, who had stopped in to sell two deer hides. "My boy's 10. Started selling furs here two years ago. A year ago he got a fisher and got $110 for it. Newt had him count it out, and when he got done, Newt said, 'Now, you gonna remember who Grandpa Newt is?'"

He will, of course. Everyone remembers Grandpa Newt.

Newton's son, Leroy, 59, owns the business now, but it is L.L. a trapper looks for when he walks through the door and lets his eyes get acquainted with the building's half-light. The old man is not hard to find. You can follow the cigar smoke to where the cloud is the thickest, or you can look for the blaze orange cap and the knee-length blue frock.

The frock hangs from L.L.'s stooped shoulders like a topcoat on a coatrack. Nothing detours it on its way to his knees. Under the frock, you see only the curled collars of a faded flannel shirt. It, too, is blue. Only a coincidence.

Inside the flannel shirt, about one button above L.L.'s belt, is the business end of Newton Furs—a zippered bank bag stuffed with currency. When you sell furs to L.L. Newton, you don't walk out with a check. You leave with real money in your pocket.

"We pay in cash, everything," L.L. says. "People like it better."

He spits into a barrel full of cowhides.

"Takes too much goddamn time to write checks in the first place," he continued. "I can pay 'em off faster than I can write a check."

Another shot of saliva into the barrel. It's as if Newton spits so a listener knows where to put the periods in the sentences.

"You're damn right they'd rather have cash," he repeats. "I think if I was a trapper, I would."

Splat. The concrete floor this time.

"Morning, sir."

A man has come through the door with two deer hides bound in twine. "You takin' deer hides?" the man asks.

"Yessir," L.L. says.

The man tosses them onto the foothills of a mountain of deer hides that has heaved up from the floor in the past few days. Leroy guesses 200 deer skins are in the pile. Many have come in this morning.

"I think they opened deer season again in the last 15 minutes, from the looks of this floor," L.L. says.

While the man waits, Newton removes the tail from each hide with two neat whacks of his knife. He tosses the tails in a box. They'll be sold to a fishing tackle manufacturer in Wisconsin. Part of all those bucktail spinners really are buck tails.

With tail, deer hides bring $5.00 at Newton Furs. Without, $4.75. L.L. slips a hand under his frock, unbuttons his shirt, retrieves the bank bag, and pulls out two five-dollar bills.

"Here you go," he says to the seller.

The man leaves, smiling. You're damn right they'd rather have cash.

No doubt the man wiped his hand on his pant leg when he got outside. The door knob is a touch greasy, animal-fat greasy. It might even have a little blood on it that will come off onto that sinewy part of your hand between your thumb and forefinger. No big deal to a trapper. His pant legs have seen worse.

From outside, the building appears to be a remodeled gas station. It is 39 feet by 39 feet, Leroy says, brown stucco over concrete block, one overhead door, one regular door, one small window around back.

A small sign—WE BUY FURS AND HIDES—is all that tells you this is the place. Trappers enter slowly, wait for their eyes to adjust, and look around.

Evidently neatness doesn't count in the fur buying trade. Furs are everywhere—dried and stacked, hanging to dry, piled, waiting to be fleshed.

Barrels of cowhides. A mountain of deer hides. Beaver blankets. Coyote hides. Muskrats. Mink. Raccoons. Foxes. Otters. Badgers. "But definitely no skunk," L.L. says. "The stink is bad enough without skunks."

"I'm not so darned sure but what skunk wouldn't smell better," Leroy says.

The furs are in every condition imaginable. Beavers, still whole, are stored in the walk-in freezer, waiting to be skinned. Other beaver are skinned, and hanging by their nostril holes on nails, waiting to be fleshed. Leroy, in his vinyl apron, is fleshing some now. More beaver blankets are nailed, 80 nails to a pelt, on plywood to dry. Finished blankets, dried and stiff-backed, are piled on the floor.

Muskrats, too many to count, hang on a wire drying. Raccoons, stretched on frames, lean against barrels of cowhide and fall over when someone walks by. More are piled along one wall, ready for shipment. Beaver castors (scent glands) dangle like miniature lungs on a wire stretched from one wall to another. The glands are valuable to perfume makers as a fixative in sweet-smelling colognes.

Though big, the room does not have floor space so much as it has aisles. The aisles are defined by the barrels, the deer hide mountain, the stacks of dried and drying furs. It is almost impossible to walk more than a few steps without something squishing underfoot. You look down. Perhaps you're standing on a raccoon tail, or a piece of fat Leroy has just fleshed off the inside of the outside of a beaver.

Bigfork twins Dan and Don Gregerson, 13, come in with their mother and 11 deer hides.

"We went around and skun 'em out for people," Don explains. The mountain grows. The cash flows. The boys smile.

"How much are 'rats (muskrats)?" Dan asks.

"Four dollars, dried," L.L. says, slipping his bank bag back into his shirt.

The boys and their mom leave.

"Those darn women that come in here don't like the smell of it," Leroy says, not missing a stroke on the beaver he's fleshing. "Probably clashes with their perfume that's made of beaver castor." He chuckles, pleased with his joke.

The phone rings.

"Newton Furs," L.L. says. Pause. "Yeah, all right." He hangs up.

"Got 400 'rats comin' in tomorrow," he announces. When the furs stack up this time of year, a security guard patrols the building. L.L. himself has been known to spend a few nights sleeping in the overstuffed chair by the door, shotgun across his lap.

Dennis Skelly, a Grand Rapids trapper, enters. He walks over to the table where L.L. is skinning mink and lays out five muskrat and three raccoon pelts. L.L. flops the furs back and forth, takes his knife and trims a piece of fat off one raccoon pelt.

"Five 'rats at $4, one 'coon at $32, one at $35, one at $30," he hollers to Picht at the desk. Picht, Newton's youngest full-timer at 18, computes the purchase.

"Hunnert and seventeen dollars," he yells back to L.L.

As the law requires, the trapper presents his trapping and small game license. Newt peels off two fifties, a ten, a five and two ones.

Skelly is pleased. "I was surprised to get $30 for the little 'coon," he said. "That's a pretty good price."

Newton furs isn't the only fur buyer in town, but Skelly always stops here first. "He gives you a pretty fair deal," he said of Newton. "He's a pretty nice old guy. My dad's known him for a long time."

Skelly puts the bills in his wallet and leaves.

L.L. goes back to skinning mink.

"The first hunderd years are the worst, I guess," he mutters. "Goddamn, I got 80 of 'em in anyway."

Splat.

Steve goes back to stretching 'coons.

Leroy flops another beaver pelt onto the fleshing beam. He hooks a nose hole over a nail and begins pushing his double-handled knife across the beaver's white skin. Globs of fat curl up, roll off, and fall to the floor. Sooner or later the trimmings end up in a barrel bound for the rendering service, where they will be sold for soap stock.

Leroy will flesh out 40 to 50 beaver hides a day, six or seven minutes per hide, plus coffee breaks.

"Somebody's gotta do it," he says. "Nobody else wants to, I don't know why. All you need's a strong back and a weak mind."

Across the room, Newt flings a mink carcass into a different barrel—more soapstock—and starts on another mink.

"The first hunderd years are the worst, they say."

Ultimately, all of the furs at Newton's will be bundled up and shipped to New York, where fur brokers will sell them to buyers from Europe and other parts of the world. The brokers must first check back with Newton's, however, to make sure the price is acceptable. If it isn't, the furs might remain in cold storage in New York for another year.

"The market is off this year," Leroy says.

"In Italy and Germany, their dollar value is decreasing compared to ours," Picht adds. "Economics have a lot to do with it."

"Supply and demand," Leroy says. He looks around the room. "Somebody's gotta buy all this junk."

A trapper, probably in his 20s, comes in wearing a camouflage coat. He's carrying a box with 19 muskrat and two mink pelts in it. He empties the box on L.L.'s table.

Silently, through the cigar smoke, L.L. appraises each. Finally, he turns and spits on the floor.

"Fifty-eight on the minks. Sixty on the 'rats," he says.

The trapper doesn't respond.

"I'm thinkin' about it here," he says in a moment. "What's that come to?"

"Hunnert and eighteen dollars," Picht answers from the desk.

"Rats gonna be 25 cents lower tomorrow," Newt says. "If you're holding any 'rats you better sell 'em to somebody today."

Slowly, the trapper reaches for his wallet. He pulls out his trapping license, then changes his mind and stuffs it away.

"I'm gonna try one more place," he says, boxing up his furs. "I'll probably be back."

He is reaching for the greasy door knob when Newt pulls the cigar from his mouth and says, "Thanks for stopping, kid."

"I'll be back," says the trapper.

Newt spits into the cowhide barrel, and gets back to skinning his mink.

Stocking Feet

The duck hunter rolls over in his bed. The radio he'd set to wake him at 3:45 a.m. is on now, and some monotone, all-night announcer is babbling some meaningless drivel the duck hunter doesn't want to hear. He staggers to his dresser and silences the announcer.

The hunter leans toward the clock dial and squints. The hands tell him it is 3:35. Why, he wonders, do alarm clocks always go off early on the nights when sleep is so precious?

He stumbles into the bathroom and turns on the water in the shower. He almost always showers before hunting trips. He isn't sure why. Too much city in him, he guesses.

He is awake, now, though. He's going to make it. He tiptoes back into the bedroom where his wife is sleeping. Most of his clothes were laid out in the living room the night before. He forgot underwear, of course, and must try to find it quietly, in the dark, so as not to wake his wife. The dresser drawer squeaks when he pulls it open. Yes, that feels like underwear.

He tiptoes back into the living room, pulling the bedroom door shut behind him. Padding around in his longjohns and wool socks, he checks the first concern of all duck hunters—the weather. He's apprehensive. The sound from outside the house bears a strong resemblance to the sound he heard in the shower —with a little wind added.

He flips on the back porch light. Rain, coming down in wind-driven sheets. Wet leaves swirl against the garage. The thought of sitting in that for several hours makes the hunter shiver. He flips the light off and makes the image disappear.

He knows his partner is up, and that he, too, has checked the weather. If they had been going grouse hunting or fishing, they would have been on the phone to see if the other still wanted to go. Duck hunters rarely make such calls.

It takes some very nasty weather to cancel a duck hunting trip. The worse the weather is, the more duck hunters like it. This is a fact not completely understood by those who remain asleep while duck hunters shuffle around the house in predawn hours.

Duck hunters won't tell you this right out, but they love that hour or so of preparation for the day's hunt. There's a coziness to it, a ritual that kindles memories from so many other good days that have begun this way. The quiet is part of it. So is the murmer of hot chocolate being heated for the thermos, and the rustle of sandwiches being made for a sack lunch.

The gear looks good piled near the door—waders, shotgun, shells, life jacket—all dry and organized. The hunter knows the sandwiches will look like an old baseball glove when he pulls them out of his duffle at mid-morning. He knows the hot chocolate won't be quite the same diluted by the raindrops that land in his thermos cup. But that will be later. The scrambled eggs and toast chase away such thoughts.

Quietly, the hunter rinses his dishes, loads his pack. He flips on the front porch light so his partner will know he's up. He waits until the last minute to put on his hunting pants and wool shirt, so he won't get too warm.

Then he tiptoes back into the bedroom and kisses his wife good-bye. It seems silly to wake her up for this, but it's part of the ritual.

He turns off lights behind him on the way to the front door. Looking out the window, he sees his partner's headlights coming up the street behind two beams of whitened raindrops. Feeling very warm inside, he steps out into the cold, wet world.

Buck Fever

Our wives didn't understand. "You're not going back to that same spot , are you?" they asked. They were talking about our deer camp, the one my Ely, Minnesota, friend Steve Piragis and I have been going to since we took up deer hunting two years ago.

We don't blame our wives for asking. We don't blame them for shaking their heads at our reply. We don't blame them because, deep down, we wonder a little bit ourselves. In the last two deer seasons, we had spent eight days at the camp hunting. We'd spent another four days scouting the area. Not an antler. Not a single white flag. Not even an apparition ghosting through the trees. Nothing. But somehow, that swampy little piece of country on the shores of the Vermilion River kept calling us back.

So, we went again. We drove the hour and a half north of Ely. Then we paddled down the river a piece, pitched our tent and fired up the cookstove.

The next morning we crawled out of our sleeping bags and went hunting.

I'd been on my stand—a hunk of granite overlooking a little valley—for about half an hour when I heard something rustling in the leaves. Must be a squirrel, I thought. Ever so slowly, I looked around. Nothing. A minute or so later, I heard more rustling. It sounded like individual footsteps. Hmmm, I thought. Must be another hunter. Surely it wasn't a deer.

Ever so slowly again, I turned to my left. Ha! Imagine that! A raccoon playing in the leaves. Looked like it might even be trying to climb up the base of an aspen tree. I watched. Right before my eyes, that raccoon became the head of a deer. I couldn't believe it. A deer. The first deer I'd ever seen in three hunting seasons. A living, breathing deer, not 40 yards away, munching on twigs. This was a historic moment.

I started looking for antlers. I couldn't see any. Too much brush. No problem. The deer started walking right in my direction.

I kept looking for little spike antlers. I was looking too low. This deer had antlers all over his head. They stuck clear up in the air. This wasn't just a deer. It was a buck, and not just any old buck, a nice buck.

I pulled back the hammer on the lever-action rifle. The hammer made a quiet click, but the buck hadn't heard it. He just kept walking my way.

It is now time for a word about heart rates. We are talking here about rapid acceleration. The buck was now about halfway to me. He paused behind a downed balsam for a moment, then he just kept coming. He was walking along, nose to the ground. He was going to walk past me about 15 feet away.

I couldn't believe it. This was just like in the stories. Then it occurred to me I had a small problem. There was nothing between this buck and me except cool November air. We were on almost the same level, and my rifle was still on my lap.

I was afraid to raise the gun because I thought the buck would see me. This sent my heart rate up to another plateau.

As the buck continued toward me, I realized I was breathing out loud. Remember how you used to breathe when you were playing hide and seek and you'd just sprinted around the house and ducked in the window well and you were out of breath but you were trying to be quiet so your sister couldn't find you? Then you understand my problem.

As I sat there, breathing out loud, heart thumping against my blaze orange jacket, gun across my lap, that deer walked right up in front of me. Fifteen feet away, broadside to me, he stopped, looked up and stared right at me.

For the next 15 seconds—or was it two days?—that beautiful buck and I stared at each other. I remember the black of his nostrils, the white hair of his muzzle and the brown of his face. His eyes were bigger than the yolks of the eggs I'd had for breakfast. And those antlers—they were all over the place.

Twice he gave me that up-and-down head movement whitetails make when they're trying to get a fix on something. But mostly he just stared.

I figured he was getting antsy and that he wasn't likely to just stroll away. I thought he'd bolt any second. I made my move.

Very slowly I began to raise my rifle off my lap. The rifle was about two inches off my lap when the buck dropped his antlers and in one motion threw them over his left shoulder. His body followed in an arc that a pole vaulter would have envied.

He landed at a gallop about 10 feet behind the spot where he'd been standing a second before. I don't know where my shot went.

The buck paused about 40 yards away and looked back at me. I don't know where that shot went either. I just know it didn't find the buck.

He no longer seemed alarmed. He simply trotted up the ridge and walked off into a deer story that will be told for many, many years by a very humble hunter.

Death and Life

He was just a kid when it happened, maybe 13 or 14.

The gun was probably the old single-shot .410-gauge, the one with the hammer that he was always afraid he might not pull back far enough, resulting in quick-fire. But this time he must have done everything right. When he touched off the little shotgun, the rabbit quit running.

He remembers it all so clearly—standing in the ditch, shooting across the pasture, watching the cottontail run away.

But he remembers best what followed. The rabbit didn't die. The shot had caught it in the hindquarters, and its back legs went limp. The rabbit tried to continue running. It pulled itself forward on its front legs. The hind legs dragged.

The hunter remembers the terror he felt, running toward the rabbit. The distance couldn't have been more than a few yards, but it seemed to take forever.

And the squealing. He's not sure just when that started. It might have been while the rabbit was trying to escape. Breathless, the boy crushed the rabbit's head under his boot to put it out of its misery. Only then had the squealing been silenced. The boy stood there, panting, relieved, shaking, ashamed, sick. The boy was me.

He was learning a lesson about hunting. He was learning that hunting isn't always pretty, that death is an undeniable and necessary part of it, that death is sometimes ugly.

He never tells the story. He hesitates to tell it now, partly because it reminds him of that feeling in his stomach, partly because he's afraid of how those who don't hunt will react.

Ultimately it is how one deals with this issue of death that determines whether he or she will continue to hunt. It is more easily accepted as a part of the hunt if one grows up tagging along with a parent who hunts. Hey, dad does it. It must be OK.

But eventually, the hunter must make that decision for himself or herself, saying, on some level, "Yes, I'm making a conscious decision to kill a living creature."

It is often made within the larger framework of a hunting season and with an awareness of the population of a given species. The hunter recognizes that a certain number of ruffed grouse or white-tailed deer or rabbits can be taken by hunters each year, and that the population will remain stable.

Such a rational approach tends to desensitize the matter. The hunter is part of a greater plan, acceptable within the eyes of game managers and game wardens and fellow hunters. The rabbit killed is not so much a single rabbit as it is part of a larger picture.

All this is fine—until the rabbit squeals, or the whitetail thrashes mindlessly in the brush, or the wing-shot grouse huddles on the forest floor, head up, eyes blinking, awaiting its fate. And the hunter must deal again with this matter of death.

This hunter would like to think such moments, if we let them, help us understand ourselves a little better. Perhaps these situations put life itself into better perspective.

Why did this animal have to suffer? Why did my grandfather who was claimed by cancer have to suffer?

Did the ruffed grouse that fell to my gunshot die with less dignity than the one claimed by the goshawk's talons? Did the neighbor's boy who perished in an auto accident die with less dignity than the soldier killed in the war?

Whose cry is more plaintive? The Canada goose honking as it searches the night skies in vain for its mate, or the widow sobbing at the window, mourning the loss of her husband?

If a hunter is sensitive, hunting offers these kinds of questions. The answers we give them might help us better understand the complexities of death—and life.

Winter/

Dancing with a River
The Last Run
Once is Enough

Dancing with a River

I'm not sure Dave wanted to go. On our way up the North Shore of Lake Superior, he kept looking out the back window of the station wagon. He seemed to be looking toward Duluth and home and the warmth we'd left behind.

Dave is the part-black-Lab, part-Irish-setter rug that adorns our kitchen floor. Sometimes he gets up and takes one of us for a walk.

On this January morning, I thought he might want to go for a ski up the Split Rock River, but he had a point with his longing look toward home. Depending on which radio weather report you listened to, the wind chill was either 40, 45, or 48 below zero. The temperature was a more sane 10 below.

But I needed this trip. I needed blue sky and a cold wind on my cheek and blood pumping through arteries. I needed the whisper of skis on snow and the chink of pole-plants on ice and the wonder of whatever else I would find.

And I needed a partner. So Dave, thinking maybe we were going to the grocery store for more Milk Bones, came along.

By the time we pulled over at the wayside rest, Dave had me thinking of home, too. The wind buffeted the little car, and cold seeped through the door where it usually didn't.

This is the tough part of any outing—the transition period. It's that in-between land where you slip from artificial warmth to body-generated heat, or from clean to dirty, or dry to wet, depending on the season.

I had dressed right—that much I knew—polypropylene, wool, windpants, pile vest, bunting jacket, mountain parka, pile cap, gaiters and Thinsulate overbooties for the ski boots.

I unloaded Dave, and we committed ourselves to the cold. The river was solid ice a hundred yards or so upstream from its confluence with Lake Superior. The old wooden Bonna skis flailed on the ice patches until they found snow. Then they creaked and hissed into an easy rhythm.

Dave bounded ahead on the light snow cover. Somehow he knew a river was down there somewhere. Instinctively, he skirted spots where the ice seemed too resonant.

We both settled on a reasonable pace. Gradually I began to realize I wasn't cold, and hadn't been. Down in this valley the wind couldn't find us, and my steady movement neutralized the 10-below-zero chill.

I had left my jacket and vest in my packsack, and was skiing in only polypropylene, a wool shirt, and the mountain parka shell. I soon found myself opening my shell to offset the additional warmth my body was producing. I had made the transition.

In its first few bends above the lake, the Split Rock is a mellow river. Then it begins to climb through minicanyons where cedars seem to grow out of pure rock, and waterfalls have long since frozen in midplunge.

None of these is on the scale of the falls on the Gooseberry, and most are negotiable without removing skis. Dave took one look at the first set, heard the Split Rock gurgling somewhere beneath all those mounds of ice, and promptly headed back toward the highway.

I took off my skis and carried him across the section that had spooked him. Once on top, he peered down quizzically as if to say, "C'mon. What's taking you so long?"

On and up we went, past deer tracks and wolf droppings and mouse burrowings.

We climbed one set of falls after another, each affording a plummeting, white sweep of the river framed by cedars and aspen. The falls themselves were jumbled humps of ice, now covered by snow. Each set presented a challenge in navigation. Like a climber planning his next move, I surveyed the falls, chose a course and herringboned or sidestepped up to the next plateau.

Only once, near the lip of a falls, did the ice give way under my weight. For most of a second, I thought I would die, until my skis came to rest on a second—and solid—layer of ice beneath.

"Close one there, Davey," I said.

But Dave was more interested in some tracks at the river's edge.

An hour or more into our ski, the river began to level out again. We were still climbing, but we had passed the falls section. At an inviting bend in the river, where the north shore caught full sunlight and offered protection from the wind, we stopped for lunch. Well, I stopped for lunch. Dave stopped to bite ice from between his pads.

With birch bark and some balsam twigs, I kindled a fire, leaned against an aspen, and opened my packsack. I ate a semi-frozen peanut-butter sandwich that looked more like a worn seat cushion, sharing bites with Dave. He didn't seem as interested in my orange or my apple cider. He would have liked to share my candy bar, but I had to invoke a double standard.

"This wouldn't be good for you," I explained.

He didn't lose interest until the last bite had disappeared into my mouth.

Lunch was quick. Even in the full sunlight, 10 below zero is 10 below zero. We left our intimate table for two overlooking the water, and moved on up the river.

When we'd been skiing upstream for two hours, we turned around and began the long run back to the car. Immediately, the difference was apparent. The long stretches that had seemed flat on the way up were actually gentle downhills now. The snow was too cold to be fast, but the going was easy. I followed the trail I'd broken on the way up, and each stride seemed longer than the one before it.

Poor Dave. Without skis he couldn't appreciate the difference. He even seemed spookier about the ice, and sometimes would lag behind as if unsure to go on. I'd ski back, reassure him or lead him across some rough ice, and away we'd go.

If the gentle runs were fast, the falls were intoxicating. Most were skiable if you stopped at the top, picked your course, and dug in your edges. Hoop, holler, and let 'er rip. Now we were having some fun.

Invariably, Dave would scoot down half the run ahead of me, then sit and wait, which meant he had several close-up looks at a pair of careening skis and flailing poles flying past him just inches away.

As I committed myself at the lip of these runs, I thought this must be how the river feels. It flows serenely to the brink of the falls, then plunges over the edge, picking its way among the rocks, slashing and dancing and sliding into the pool below.

It might eddy about for a moment or two. Then slowly the river gathers momentum and approaches the next drop, where the madness and folly deliver it once again to the landing below.

Again and again, we made our descents, Dave hesitating, myself in reckless abandon, until finally the Split Rock spit us out near the big lake.

Reason would have told us not to make the trip—too cold, too windy, too risky to go without a skiing companion. Perhaps reason was right.

We hadn't challenged the elements and won. We had simply taken what we were given, treated it with respect and worked within our limits. Along the way we had discovered a wild river and felt the spirit of its dance.

The Last Run

It sounded so simple.

"Would you like to run a team in the Beargrease Sled Dog Race?" they asked. "Not all 350 miles of it. Just up to Finland, 70 miles or so. Enough to get a feel for the race."

"Sure," I said.

Next thing I knew it was a Tuesday afternoon in early December, and I was standing on a dogsled in Lloyd Gilbertson's yard. This was my first training run.

Five Alaskan huskies were leaping madly in their traces, trying to pull the sled free. But the snow hook, a grappling-style steel claw, was buried in packed snow, and I had all of my 158 pounds planted on it.

Lloyd ran back from his seven-dog team and shouted at me over the din. "Give me a count of five or ten before you come. That way if I don't make the haw at the end of the drive, we won't get messed up."

"Right," I hollered back.

"Haw" is sled-dog talk for a left turn, as opposed to "gee," which is a right turn.

Lloyd pulled his hook, bounced over a snowbank, and disappeared around a bend in the driveway. I had counted to one when my dogs ripped the hook out of the ground with me on it.

I managed to grab the sled's handlebar and hop on the runners. I didn't stay there long. By the time we cleared the snowbank the sled was at a 45-degree angle, and it was on its side a second later. I held on as we raced down the driveway, like a water-skier who had fallen but wouldn't let go of his tow rope. When we hit another bank and I became a human snowplow blade, I decided to let go.

Meanwhile, Lloyd's team didn't make its haw. My dogs caught his before I caught my sled, and we had ourselves a 12-dog tangle in the makings.

Somehow, Lloyd made sense from the mess and we were on the way. Well, for a minute we were. Lloyd stopped his team a quarter of a mile up the trail and turned around to see how I was doing. By the time he turned around to check his team again, it was too late. Toivo, his lead dog, had found Tula, a female in heat, too irresistible. We were in for a five-minute time-out.

And it had sounded so simple.

Driving a dog team is somewhat like driving a stage coach with no reins. The dogs are hitched two-by-two along the gangline, except for the lead dog, who stands alone at the head of the pack. Each dog wears a harness and a collar. Tug lines, the ones the dogs pull on, are snapped to the back of the harnesses, just above each dog's tail. A short neck line is clipped to each dog's collar. Except for ol' Toivo, the lead dog. He's just hitched by the tug line. His front end is free to go anywhere it wants and it often does.

The sled is a wood and plastic toboggan affair that weighs about 30 pounds. It has a simple brake that is part steel bar, part bungee cord. Sometimes, depending on snow conditions, it works.

The snow hook is your emergency brake, designed to hold the sled on longer stops. You just drop it in the snow and stomp it down. Sometimes, depending on snow conditions, it works.

I learned something about all of this on my second outing behind the dogs. That was the day we met the junkyard dog.

The junkyard is a mile or two from Lloyd's home, as the dogs run. I was running seven dogs with Toivo out front, and Lloyd was running a shorter team behind me.

"Let me catch up to you before we get to the junkyard," Lloyd had said. "Sometimes that's kind of exciting."

Well, the junkyard is on the Cramer Road, which is snowpacked, hard as a rock, and fast. Don't think Toivo and the gang didn't know who was riding their sled. Running someone else's dog team is kind of like being the substitute teacher. Remember what you did to the substitute teacher?

We were flying down the road, and I was standing on the brake, which did nothing more than make the ride rough. I remember looking back at Lloyd, way back. Toivo never hesitated. He barreled past a slowly decaying truck in the junkyard driveway and headed right for the junkyard dog, a German shepherd the color of a rusted fender.

The next moments run together in my memory. I recall a lot of growling, a lot of my yelling "Whoa!" and Don the junkyard man standing on the porch of his trailer house saying calmly, "They don't listen, do they?"

We inched ever closer to the junkyard dog before I finally managed to wedge the sled's brushbow behind a truck bumper. I ran up, grabbed Toivo, led him out of the yard, and off we went.

The rest of that 25-mile run was somewhat less exciting, except that Toivo was more interested in Tula than in running straight ahead.

I might have been out there still had it not been for a couple of Lake County highway maintenance men who interrupted their lunch break to hold Toivo and the sled while I sorted out a massive tangle by County Road 8.

And it had sounded so simple.

Then there was Brandy. On my next training run he was sitting there in the middle of the road, just past the junkyard. Brandy is a shaggy little dog about the size of a country mailbox. Sled dogs don't like dogs that aren't in a harness.

Don't misunderstand. Sled dogs aren't vicious. I'd have any of Gilbertson's as a house pet. But when a team of dogs is hitched up, they'll chase anything that isn't.

You remember the junkyard road. Hardpack. I saw Brandy 200 yards ahead and hopped on the brake with both feet. We kept picking up speed. I threw down the hook. It just jangled on the snowpack. I was no match for nine dogs.

As soon as I saw him, I started yelling at Brandy. Toivo seemed to think I was urging him on. It might have been the fastest I've ever traveled behind a dog team.

We caught Brandy before he cleared the snowbank. It was ugly. Brandy's owner, Dave Grinstead, came running across the frozen Baptism River from his cabin swinging a broken canoe paddle at the dogs. I welcomed his arrival.

I had set the hook in the snowbank and jumped into the melee myself. I remember teeth and fur and low growls and three dogs' jaws locked on Brandy at one time. Grinstead kept swinging. I kept prying jaws apart.

I stuck my hand in the middle of the mess once and it wouldn't come out. I yanked again. My hand came out, minus a finger on my glove.

Then, for an instant, Brandy was free. I tossed him out of the mess onto the snow-covered ice of the river. Grinstead was a saint. He held my sled while I untangled dogs. He asked me to come by sometime for a cup of coffee. You meet some fine people in some unusual ways.

Brandy spent two nights at the Lake County Veterinary Clinic. Lots of lacerations, but he made it. Lloyd picked up the bill.

And it had seemed so simple.

A five-day camping trip with the dogs over the New Year's weekend helped define our relationship. Toivo and I began to understand—even respect—each other. I was no longer the substitute teacher.

Then, four days before the race, on a crystal Sunday evening, I drove north to make my last training run. This one would be at night, to simulate race conditions.

Lloyd dropped me off with nine dogs on the North Shore Trail, a snow-machine trail that undulates through the woods near Finland, Minnesota. The John Beargrease Sled Dog Race would be held on the same trail.

A crescent moon hung in the west like an alabaster apostrophe. The dogs ran as if possessed, up the hills, down the hills, across frozen creekbeds. Moonshadows played upon the snow. It was magic.

For the first time, I felt in control. When we stopped, the snow hook held in the packed snow. Toivo held the lines tight until I was ready to go again.

We made a wrong turn, but once I pointed Toivo in the right direction, we were sailing again. I was giddy. I rocked back on the sled runners to watch the stars go by. I praised each dog as we ran.

Finally, I could be excited about the race itself. No longer was I apprehensive. I was ready.

I'm not sure how I lost the sled. We were careening down a long hill 20 miles into our run. We were less than three miles from Gilbertson's. I had stepped on the brake to slow the sled. We swerved, hit the snowbank, and the sled was on its side.

I hung on as long as my mittened hands would hold, but was soon stripped from the sled. I yelled once at the dogs. Then I was alone.

I couldn't believe it. One moment a perfect run; the next, an embarrassment—to say nothing of a long walk.

The dogs wouldn't stop until they became tangled. That much I knew. I hoped they'd run across a fresh set of moose tracks and get sidetracked. No such luck.

I walked a couple of miles before I came to the asphalt road that led to Gilbertson's, a mile away. I found no dog tracks on the snowmobile trail across the road, so I started walking toward Gilbertson's.

At the William Mudgett home I stopped to call Gilbertson. No answer. I hoped the dogs had run on home, and that Lloyd was out in the yard with them. No such luck.

By 8 p.m. I tracked Lloyd down. He smiled, put his arm around me and said, "Welcome to the club."

We began looking for the dogs. We looked by car. We looked by flashlight. We enlisted Dick Nikula and his snowmobile. At midnight we still hadn't found them. I drove home.

Gilbertson found the dogs early the next morning. It wasn't pretty. Toivo and Rado had fought. Toivo was cut badly on his left ear.

That wasn't the worst, Gilbertson told me when he called. I can still hear his words, coming slowly and quietly from the other end of the line.

"We lost Sonja," he said. Sonja, the tiniest dog on the team, 35 pounds of heart, pure white and beautiful.

"We lost Sonja." "We lost Sonja." The words wouldn't go away.

She'd been caught in the tangle. A broken neck, Gilbertson said. We lost Sonja.

Nothing mattered anymore. The race was already out of the question. Toivo wouldn't be ready. But at least he would heal.

We lost Sonja.

And it had sounded so simple.

Once is Enough

The snow fleas were everywhere. Little black flecks, like elongated pepper, littered the top of the snow on the portage. I stopped, bent over and nudged one of the fleas with the steel tip of my ski pole. The fleck disappeared. It had flexed the flipping appendage beneath its tiny black fuselage and—*flit*—it was gone. It reappeared somewhere within the sphere of my sight, but I couldn't tell where. Now it was just another snow flea.

I would have told someone about the snow fleas, but nobody else was there. I was alone under the early March sun on this portage between Snowbank Lake and Parent Lake, east of Ely, Minnesota. Alone in the quiet of late winter in the Boundary Waters Canoe Area Wilderness. Alone among thousands of snow fleas.

I lurched ahead on the packed trail, lugging my sled full of winter camping gear behind.

I'd been planning a trip like this for a couple of years. I had wondered what it would be like to travel solo in the winter woods. It was enjoyable enough with a group of four or eight or ten, or behind a couple of dog teams, but I kept telling myself I ought to try it alone someday.

I'm not sure what I was after. I'm not a solitary person by nature. I wasn't looking for a personal challenge that would reveal my true inner self. Maybe I just wanted to see if I could do it—whatever that meant.

So on that winter weekday I'd loaded my sled with tent, sleeping bag, campstove, ice chisel, photo gear, food, and fishing tackle. On cross-country skis, I had set off from Snowbank Lake, heading in the direction of Thomas Lake, some nine or ten miles to the east. I had given myself three days.

The trail was firm and fast, packed by the skis and sleds of several other parties following this informal route in quest of Thomas Lake's trout. It was after 1 p.m. when I left the landing. I didn't figure I could cover the distance into Thomas that day.

Purple ski wax was just right, so the temperature must have been around 30. The sled fairly flew behind me on the lakes. The portages were a different story. Unable to get sufficient traction on the uphills, I'd shed my skis and walk.

The sled balked on the grades. Its waist belt felt like two arms around me, trying to haul me down backwards. As soon as I was over a crest, the sled grew impatient, pushing me down the hills with the stiff fiberglass wands attached to the waist harness.

A woodpecker welcomed me to Parent Lake. A mile later I circumvented the open water of an incoming creek and attacked the portage into Disappointment Lake. On I moved, across the two miles of Disappointment, into the swamps and small lakes that would lead to Thomas.

I stopped twice for energy nuggets—homemade spheres of oats, butter, molasses, brown sugar, and honey. I tossed down water. I was skiing in long-john tops and khaki pants with long-john bottoms. That and a pair of earmuffs were all I needed. My ski gloves seemed too warm.

My companions in the afternoon were two Canada jays, one squirrel, and some moose tracks.

By 4:15 I was weary and almost to Thomas Lake. I didn't want to push myself, so I put on snowshoes and broke trail to the protection of some jack pines and spruce at the edge of a frozen swamp. The snow was deep. Off the trail, it was knee-high. Snowshoes were mandatory. Pitching a tent, alone, in snowshoes isn't easy.

In the fading afternoon, I gathered wood from the dead lower branches of a spruce. I dug out a coffee pot and began melting snow for water over the campstove. I retrieved a Kraft Egg Noodle and Chicken dinner from my food pack. Mmmmm, mmmmm.

One of the best things about having companions along on winter trips is that the work load is spread among everyone. A couple of people can pitch the tent while someone else plans dinner and a few others gather firewood.

This solo thing was a circus. I added more snow to the melting water. I tossed my sleeping bag in the tent. I gathered more wood. I read the box dinner directions. I dug out my headlamp. I added more snow to the melting water. I gathered more wood.

By 6 p.m. I was sitting at the edge of my tent, slurping down the slippery egg noodles and sauce. Light was fading. For some reason I looked up toward the trail I'd skied in on. I was startled to see two men standing there. They were behind a dogsled hitched to five dogs. Behind them were three other small sleds, tied in single file.

"Howdy," I said. It felt strange to be talking. "Care for a cup of tea?" I asked.

"No, we're on our way out," said one man.

They had caught fish on Thomas. Yes, I was alone. Nice travelin' weather. Almost too warm. They were from Embarrass. I was from Duluth. Two of the trout were six-pounders. There were some boughs cut on the point just before the two islands at the far end of Thomas if I wanted them for my tent—wood, too.

Silences between the subjects served as paragraph indentations. I grew accustomed to my voice again. It was good to be talking to someone.

When the silences grew longer than the paragraphs, the men said they'd be going. One of them spoke to the lead dog. Without a sound, the column moved down the trail and out of sight around a bend.

My egg noodles were cold.

After boiling water for tea, I shut off the stove. The evening was full of quiet. Many times—on the trail and in camp—I stopped and listened to it. Not a branch bending or a bird chatting or a leaf skittering. Just quiet. I could hear my heartbeat in my ears and my chest at the same time. I liked that.

What I'd have liked more is to turn to someone who was doing dishes, maybe, and say, "Stop. Just listen for a minute." And we'd have listened to the quiet together.

I lit my fire and watched it begin its vertical descent through a cylinder of snow. The spruce seemed eager to burn, to release the energy of all those years storing up sunlight on that shoreline.

I wrote in my notebook, painting broad lines of graphite onto the white sheets with a blunt pencil, angling the notebook toward the fire for more light. I was sitting in my empty sled, snowshoes still on my feet.

I thought about the way I had left home—in a hurry, as usual, with last-minute details at work, and discussions at home. Why did it have to be that way so often? Was life really so complicated? Were we trying to do too much in too little time?

I tossed a few more sticks of spruce on the fire.

I missed my sweeties—the one who was 37 and the one who was one. I sang them a song. I sounded lonely. I thought about heading for home in the morning. Forget the fish. What's a six-pound lake trout compared to a 23-pound cuddler?

I let the fire go low, then orange, then gray, drowning in its own meltwater. It was 7:45 p.m., time for bed.

I awoke in the dark listening to a thousand tiny tappings on the tent. It sounded like a snow flea sock hop. I knew better. It was snowing. Throughout the night the snow accumulated atop the tent, then slumped down the sides of the fly to the ground.

By morning my sled and food pack were just visible. The coffee pot wore a white cap. Snow was still falling. I had remembered the wind blowing for a time during the night.

I snowshoed out to the main trail to see what condition it was in. What I saw didn't please me. The trail was just discernible, a slight depression of white on a field of more white. If I were going to have decent travel, I needed to see that trail.

That was all the impetus I needed. I would head back for civilization instead of continuing to Thomas. I wasn't sure I could get out in one day anyway, breaking trail in that snow.

Breakfast was oatmeal, eaten right from the cook pot. I melted a quart of water for the trail and laced it with Tang. I packed up. At 8:15 I moved out.

The sky had begun to lighten, and soon the snow stopped. The gray lifted, and world was brilliant in blue and white. The spruce wore the new snow on latticework boughs. The white pines bore their snow in round clumps, like handfuls held forward in offering.

I could have appreciated all of this more if the sled hadn't been acting like a four-bottom John Deere plow. For some reason, it was listing to the right, digging into the snow and the wall of the remnant trail.

I stopped once to shift the sled's weight. I stopped again to inspect its base and scrape some frost from it. The frost looked harmless enough, but created the effect of sandpaper on downhill skis. That's what made the sled dig in.

Scraping helped. The sled pulled more easily, but still nothing like it had on well-packed trail. After the trip I weighed my gear and discovered I had been pulling 135 pounds. At the time it was better not knowing.

I wasn't skiing. I was walking on skis. I glided only on short downhills in the woods between swamps and lakes, and then slowly. Gone was the previous day's packed-track exhilaration. This was work.

The sun rose higher, and I squinted harder. The day was going to be too warm. I could almost feel the snow begin to moisten and compact. The more it settled, the less the sled liked it.

I reached Disappointment Lake—a four-mile ski—by 10:30. Already my legs were tired. I stopped for a lunch break, sharing two Polish sausages, whole wheat buns, tea, and half a Milky Way with two Canada jays.

Under the midday sun I hitched up and moved on. I thought a lot about dog-team travel, and how right it seems for this country. I thought of all the dogsleds I'd ridden on, watching dogs work so that I could ride free. Now I was the dog.

A hundred yards onto Disappointment, the remnant trail vanished. It was there, somewhere, under the smooth plane of white, but I couldn't find it. I'd stop and poke for it with my ski poles. Nothing. I'd look ahead, trying to see the row of filled-in pole holes that had guided me thus far. Nothing. Frustrated, I began skiing side to side, trying to feel for the trail with my skis. I would stumble onto it, only to lose it a few yards beyond.

It depressed me to look back at my S-curve wanderings. I had two miles of this lake to lick.

The snow began to gather under my ski boots and freeze to my bindings. I couldn't stand flat on my skis. I rolled off them left and right in soft snow.

The sled began icing again and digging in on its side. I scraped the sled. The scraping helped for maybe 10 minutes. I swore at the sled. That didn't help at all.

If I'd been traveling with someone else, I'd have been breaking trail only half the time. With three of us, only a third of the time. I had a lot of time to think about that.

Somewhere near the end of Disappointment I found the trail again. The sled was plowing, but I wouldn't scrape it until I reached the portage. I sat on the sled, sweating freely, munching energy nuggets, and drinking without reservation because I knew I'd cross a creek on the portage.

We won't talk about Parent Lake, about the disappearing trail, about thinking I'd overshot the portage, about skiing an extra half-mile to double-check, about realizing I was 50 yards from the portage when I'd begun to doubt myself.

Dark clouds began to build in the west. The wind, still at my back, began to feel cooler. I was tired, empty. I could always spend another night on the trail, but I didn't want to if I didn't have to. I was still a 300-yard portage and one and a half miles of lake from my car.

I had felt this way before—in a cross-country ski race that I'd begun too fast, on a two-mile portage through Manitoba muskeg, on Great Slave Lake during a 50-mile day with a dog team and skis.

I plodded over the portage. I walked down onto Snowbank. I could see from the portage that the trail was visible only in the protected area near shore, then—unbroken white.

I popped a nugget and shoved on. I had to round a large island, then a small island, then cover another half mile to the landing.

The trail was nowhere. I quit seeking it, shuffling on through 15 inches of soft snow in the most direct line of travel. Each energy nugget took me a little less farther down the trail than the last. I felt a little light-headed. I threw on a jacket to retain more body heat.

I remembered hypothermia stories, and how the victims rarely knew it was happening to them. I didn't want to be a hypothermia story. I made the big island. I made the small island.

Ahead I could see the broad patch of white that was the landing. I was determined to get there. I stopped for another nugget and more water.

Then it occurred to me: take off those skis and put on those snowshoes. It couldn't be any worse. It might be better.

It was—not a lot, but a little.

Seventy-five steps. Rest. Seventy-five more. Rest. The landing loomed larger. I stared it down as I strode on. Three or four more rests and I was there.

It felt so good to stop.

After I'd loaded up, I sat in the car with the heater running. I ate three whole-wheat buns. I ate a Hershey bar with almonds. I drank the rest of my water.

As I sat there, I thought about this solo winter camping. I was glad I'd tried it, because only by trying it did I learn something. I learned that it's something I'll probably never do again.

I put the car in gear and headed home to see my sweeties.

Spring/

Gearing Up
Back on the Brule
Pick of the Litter
Fishing Partners

Gearing Up

I pulled the tackle box out of the basement cabinet. Its familiar heft felt good in my hand. I took the box upstairs, set it on the table and opened its plastic lid.

It was time to start dreaming about fishing season, time to forget the March snowstorm that was raging outside my window and transport myself to another time, another place, another world, which I did the moment I folded back that amber lid.

There they were. Rapalas. Tiny Torpedoes. Flatfish. They were just where I'd left them after last summer, lying there, ready and resplendent in their fluorescent oranges, electric blues, and natural silvers.

Don't get the wrong idea. This isn't one of those suitcase-size tackle boxes with tray upon telescoping tray. This is your basic Mini-Magnum Side-Kick, about the size of a school kid's lunch box. It's the only way to go when you have to put your tackle in a packsack to get to the lakes you fish.

The backcountry angler can't afford the organized luxury of one lure per tackle box slot, of course. My orange and black Flatfish shares a tray with a green fish-scale Tiny Torpedo and a gold floating Rapala.

I picked up the Rapala. The Torpedo and the Flatfish came with it, dangling from alternate ends of the Rapala like a mobile. A canoe angler learns to live with such treble-hook trauma. Across from the plugs were the smaller slots with split-shot sinkers, egg sinkers, and single hooks.

I stared at that tackle for a while and found myself wishing I could do something besides just look at it. When I was a kid, before my leanings had turned from baseball to fishing, I'd pull my ball glove out of the closet when it was time to start dreaming of spring.

Now, that was dream fodder. You could put the glove on, feel the cracked and sweat-stained leather in the finger slots, toss a ball into the pocket of the glove, feel that satisfying slap of horsehide on leather. You could lie on the bed, flat on your back, tossing that ball up to the ceiling and swallowing it with the mitt on its return trip.

You can't do that sort of thing with fishing tackle. You can't very well tie on a swivel, snap on a Tiny Torpedo, and wing it across the living room. You can't even go outside and flip a Rapala out by the clothesline—not in the fury of a March blizzard, not while maintaining any respect in the neighborhood, anyway.

A tackle box doesn't even smell. If I couldn't find a ball to smack into the pocket of my old baseball glove, I could always put the mitt up to my nose and inhale that delicious aroma. That wasn't just leather. That was sunshine and dirt and sweat. But all I had was tackle, just lying there.

So I sat and stared, and remembered. I looked at that jointed Rapala, the J-9 in gold and black.

Suddenly I was up on Shelley Lake in Ontario's Quetico Provincial Park. We were paddling through a narrows, trolling the Rapala. We'd just passed an island where three men were breaking camp. That's when the smallmouth bass made his move.

I dropped to my knees to keep the line tight as I set the hook. Then I held on for the battle. The bass went crazy. He flopped. He leaped. He tore line from my reel.

It was several minutes before I slipped my thumb into his jaw, removed the hook, and lifted him over the gunwale. As I did, the three campers on the island broke into quiet applause. They'd been watching the whole incident. I smiled and waved.

The fish was three and a half or four pounds, thick on the sides and deep in the belly. We put him on the stringer and kept paddling.

Two slots over from the jointed Rapala in the tackle box was a smaller Rapala, fluorescent orange across the back, gold on the sides. It had fooled a three-pound rainbow on a small canoe-country lake a couple of springs ago. I'll always remember it. It's the lure that was on my wife's line, in the rainbow's jaw, and in the dog's tail all at the same time.

I was trying to sort all of that out with a small pair of scissors. When the dog's tail wagged, the fish would flop, which would make the dog want to jump to the far side of the canoe.

Well, the dog lived, and the canoe didn't swamp, and the fish tasted great that night. But it had been touchy for a while.

I flipped the tackle box over. The other side was mostly Mepps spinners, rubber-bodied jigs, Corkies and cheap spoons. Where were all those good lake trout spoons? Had I squirreled them away in a winter tackle box, or would I need to replenish my supply? And swivels. Where do all those swivels go over the winter? There must be swivel-eating bugs that live wherever fishing tackle is stored. They hibernate all summer and come out only at nights in the winter. They flatten themselves to almost nothing, slither under the lids of tackle boxes and gorge themselves on swivels. How they get out, I have no idea.

I made a mental note: lake trout spoons, swivels.

I know what will happen. I'll get to the tackle shop and get carried away. I'll need more Fuzz-E-Grubs, especially in chartreuse. I'll need extra rubber jig bodies. I'll need some spinner blades. I might even need another tackle box, just a small one. The

smaller they get, the cuter they are. And line. I'll need new line
for my reels.

I closed the tackle box. It had served its purpose. I was beyond
the dreaming stage. I had moved on to gearing up.

Go on, March, I thought. Get this snow out of your system,
because one of these nights the peepers are going to be calling in
the woods across the street. The marsh marigolds are just waiting
to burst through to daylight. The ice is starting to rot, down
where we can't see it yet. One of these days, not so very long
from now, fishing season is going to come again.

And I'm going to be ready.

Back on the Brule

It wouldn't be a long paddle—three, maybe four miles. But it would be enough. Enough to feel the pull of moving water again, to see some steelhead on their spawning beds, to rejuvenate a soul badly in need of spring.

Not just any river can deliver those goods. All are moving this time of year, of course, but many are too rowdy in their swollen exuberance to let a canoeist tag along.

Lots of them take a run of steelhead from Lake Superior, but many of those are too cloudy in their runoff roil to let you see the fish.

Most rivers, it seems, have to shout about the arrival of spring, but Wisconsin's Brule finds no need for all the clamor. It is content, especially in its upper reaches, simply to lay the season before you. What you make of it is up to you.

I slipped the canoe into the water at Big Lake, a widening in the river about eight miles, as the river flows, above U.S. Highway 2 and the town of Brule.

This would be a solo paddle. I had tried halfheartedly and too late to line up a paddling partner. Now, drifting toward the riffle below Big Lake, I was glad to be alone. It seemed right.

The day couldn't have been finer, at least by northern Wisconsin standards for early April. Shelf ice still hung out over the shore in places, but the temperature was flirting with 50 and the sky was that kind of blue you see behind the boughs of a white pine when you close your eyes and dream of summer. It felt good to be swinging a paddle again.

A fish broke water ahead of me, just below the riffle. I had seen steelhead spawning there before and had expected to see them there again. Then the current caught me, and I was there.

Steelhead went scurrying everywhere, slithering shadows against the stream bottom. I could see their redds, the gravelly nests where they would lay their eggs.

I have seen this steelhead show several times now, and always it touches something deep within me. It is on a scale somewhere up there with watching a skein of geese winging across the heavens or observing the wild mating dance of a pair of loons. Biologists can put forth all the facts they want about these happenings, but they'll still be mystical to me.

The steelhead swimming below my canoe were safe, at least from the yarn flies of anglers. Fishing season doesn't open on the upper Brule until early May. The only worry a steelhead has this time of year is a hungry bald eagle.

Up ahead at a bend in the river I saw a man and woman relaxing on a carpet of leaves under a clump of birch trees.

"Howdy," I said.

"Howdy," said Buck Follis.

Buck's back was propped squarely against one of the birches, and his cap was slunk down over his forehead. His wife, Shirley, was hunkered beside him. Their dog, Charlie, was getting tough with a stick nearby.

The Follises were caretakers of a cabin up the hill, they said.

"We were raking the yard and decided to take a break," Shirley said.

We talked about how good the pine needles smelled, about the kind of winter the deer had, about the steelhead spawning.

"They been spawnin' for a coupla weeks already," Buck said. "You'll probably see some more in the rapids around the corner and below Lucius Lake."

I pushed off and left the Follises to their rake break.

Buck was right. A steelhead leaped in the rapids downstream, so close to the canoe that I flinched. I felt the fish thump against the bottom of the canoe as I passed through the fast water.

The riffle spit me out into Lucius Lake, another wide spot in the Brule's path to Lake Superior. My arrival startled a hooded merganser drake and hen. They burst into flight and disappeared down the lake.

I paddled along a sheet of ice that extended 50 feet over the water from the north shore of the lake. Drop by drop the ice sheet was becoming river, and what once fell from the sky would soon become part of Lake Superior.

The canoe moved on down the river, past weathered log homes and ancient cedars hanging out over the water. The wind stirred wind chimes at an unseen cabin and hissed through the delicate needles of white pines. People and nature get along well here on the Brule.

At the lower end of Lucius Lake I looked for the big white pine where I'd seen an eagle's nest before. This time, I saw no nest. I saw only the jagged stump of what once was a giant white pine, and wondered if the eagle highrise fell with the forest monarch. I was afraid I knew the answer.

On down the river.

Two pair of ducks took wing. A steelhead torpedoed by me in the shallows. A pair of hawks too high to identify soared over the valley north of the river.

I wasn't the only one moving down the river today. My company included several cedar sprigs, some bright green and others rust. For several minutes I drifted along next to a maple leaf. It was brown and curled, but rode the current as proudly as if it were a float in some aquatic parade.

The river narrowed and quickened. I looked for steelhead again. Something caught my eye off to the left of the canoe, coming my way. I thought it was a fish, but took a quick second look.

It was a muskrat, the first I'd ever seen swimming underwater. It looked like a wet wool glove with a rudder. It swam right under the canoe, headed for the other side of the river, and disappeared under the overhanging bank.

The muskrat had hardly disappeared when a shadow passed over the canoe. Instinctively, I looked toward the sun. Far above me, a large hawk was riding the breeze off Lake Superior. My bird book and I decided it was probably a rough-legged hawk.

On I paddled.

I skirted a black ash swamp and another dripping ice shelf. I thought I heard a woodpecker around the next bend, but I didn't need my bird book to identify the species when I got there. It was Roger Anderson, repairing the handrails of the Winniboujou Club bridge over the river. Anderson's pickup radio provided background music as we chatted bridge-to-boat.

Anderson had been watching the steelhead move upstream, he said. He'd seen some coming downstream, too, scarred-up after spawning. He was worried about the early May opening of fishing on this stretch of the river. Still fish spawning then, he said.

He'd also seen some big bunches of suckers, maybe 200 in a group. And four eagles. Yes, he said, the big white pine at the lower end of Lucius Lake with the eagle nest had blown down in that Fourth of July storm last summer. He thought it might have had a couple of eaglets in it when it went down. Sad deal about the eaglets.

Then Anderson got back to pounding, and I got back to paddling, past a screened-in patio, several docks, and a boathouse named "NE DODG E WON."

It was at one of these docks that I finally pulled over. I saw the sign that said "Private Property." I know I was wrong, but it was facing the sun just right, and I wasn't going to be there long.

I pulled my pack out of the canoe and folded my jacket on top of it for a pillow. Then I spread my life jacket beneath me, lay back and ate a Butterfinger and an apple. I lay there, warm and full, with my cap pulled down over my eyes.

The chickadees were chickadee-dee-deeing in the spruce. The nuthatches were bzzz-bzzz-bzzzing in the pines. I was just beginning to contemplate how clean the needles of a white pine look in spring when I was no longer contemplating anything at all.

I don't know how long I slept. I know only that it was one of those delicious, sun-on-the-face naps that everyone should be required to take at least once each spring.

I awoke slowly. The chickadees and nuthatches were still busy proclaiming the glories of chickadeedom and nuthatchdom. The river was still gurgling along the dock and boathouse.

I loaded up and moved on, down another set of riffles, through the old trestle pilings, down to the canoe landing just above the Winniboujou Bridge on County Road B.

That was enough, I figured. I didn't want to try Hall's Rapids and Little Joe Rapids by myself, not in 35-degree water.

Besides, I'd gotten what I'd come for. I'd felt the tug of a wild river again. I'd seen the steelhead spawning. I'd stolen a nap in the sun. That was enough.

Pick of the Litter

The hunter smiles almost all the time he watches her. He can't help it. Pups do that to a person, especially 12-week-old black Labrador pups.

Dakota Slough, he calls her, after the South Dakota wetlands where she'll spend some of the finest moments of her life. Kota, for short. A guy can't be reeling off four-syllable titles when he's got a rooster pheasant down and he needs his dog in a hurry.

She was pick of the litter on a western Minnesota farm. His best hunting buddy's male Lab had sired the litter and given the hunter first choice. He ruled out the four male pups because he wanted a female.

He put the four females through their paces by the book when they were seven weeks old. He picked them up by their tummies to see how they reacted. Kota squirmed just right. He held them down on their backs. She wiggled and whined. He walked them, called them to him, stroked their backs. Kota measured up, not too rambunctious, but curious and frisky.

That earned Kota her first trip across Minnesota in the little yellow pickup. She'll make many more, but they'll be different. The air will be crisp, and she'll sleep curled up on a hunting vest that smells of tailfeathers. She'll know why she's going, if not exactly where.

This spring, she knew neither. All she knew was that she missed her littermates and seemed to be moving very fast.

She was all tummy and sharp teeth then. Now she's all legs and paws. She has two speeds, the hunter says—wide open and dead asleep. Mostly, she sleeps. But when she's awake, watch out.

Already she's bringing her scruffy gray mouse back to the hunter when he tosses it. But if she decides just to chew on it instead of bringing it back, he doesn't scold her.

Her lessons now are sit, stay, heel, and come—15 minutes a day in two separate sessions. Keep the sessions short, leave her wanting more, the book says. The hunter does.

He wants to make it fun, to do nothing that would diminish her natural desire to retrieve. That's why he grins and silently grits his teeth when Kota brings him a dress shoe or a prized memento from an overseas trip. Those things happen.

The hunter smiles genuinely when he watches the pup play with the old dog. The old girl is 11 now. She's given the hunter more memorable retrieves than he ever deserved to get. She's got some white on her jowls, and she's thick across the back, not fat, just cut a little differently than she used to be.

Mostly, the old pro puts up with Kota's exuberance. She lets the pup snap endlessly at her ears. She even plays tug-of-war with the shoe a couple of times a day. When she's tired of it, she just finds a patch of sun somewhere and lies down again.

The hunter took them out together one day, down in the weeds by the grain elevators. He let the old dog get hot on a rooster's trail, the pup right alongside. When the rooster flushed and the pup jumped back in fright, he laughed out loud.

He smiled a couple of flushes later when the pup began to enjoy it. He felt good, too, letting the old dog show the youngster how it was done. He might have to help the old girl up onto the tailgate once in a while, but she's still got the nose.

He wonders if the pup will have that kind of nose. He wonders if she'll stay with the crippled mallards in a heavy chop. He wonders if she'll have the same soft mouth when she catches up with a rooster on the run.

He thinks about those things, and smiles a lot.

Fishing Partners

Kristian Jankofsky, nine, opened his green plastic tackle box. He unfolded its three tiers of trays, plucked out an orange plug with black spots on it, and snapped it onto his line.

"If there's a northern in here, he should go after this," Kristian said.

He gave the monster plug a fling with his Zebco rod and his old, black reel. The plug plunked down somewhere in the placid backwaters of Fish Lake, north of Duluth.

Another fishing season was under way for one more of about a million Minnesota anglers.

Kristian's fishing partner didn't take particular notice of the young angler's cast. Harold Ely, 65, also of Duluth, has fished with Kristian enough to know his plugs usually land in the water.

These two—Ely and Kristian—are old fishing partners. Been fishing together three or four years now, ever since Kristian was about five. That was back when he had just one tackle box.

The anglers happen to be neighbors. It's a safe bet this fishing friendship had its roots on summer evenings when Ely would return from fishing trips and Kristian would come trotting across the street to drool over the older man's catch.

They have now shared a boat many, many times. Along the way, they've taken some big fish. "Humongous fish," Kristian said. Almost everything Kristian does is humongous, in the thousands, or on some larger-than-life scale—which is to say, he has at least one quality that makes a good angler.

Ely is "Mr. Ely" to Kristian, a fourth-grader who has been taught to respect his elders. Kristian has said "Mr. Ely" so often, in fact, that the words are no longer separate. They come out something like, "Mistreely," a contraction that comes in especially handy when one has a fish on, or thinks he has a fish on, or needs the needle-nosed pliers in a hurry.

Mistreely says he fishes with Kristian "for company, mostly." But the observer suspects that when one has three grandchildren, the nearest in Denver and the farthest in Hawaii, that Kristian represents more than good company.

It was about two plug casts past 9 a.m. on Fish Lake. A wool shirt was too warm, and the sky was nearly cloudless. Minnesota openers don't come any nicer.

Ely and Kristian putted around the cove off the Bachelor's Road landing on the lake. The 4-horsepower Evinrude pushed Ely's spotless, 14-foot Alumacraft at just the right speed to entice a walleye. But Kristian was dreaming of northerns.

"Mistreely, remember that one time we were fishing on Rice Lake and my minnow was just dangling over the water and that northern came up and ate it?" Kristian asked.

"Yeah," Ely said.

That was typical of a conversation between the two. Mostly, they went about the business of fishing. Kristian hoped for a northern. Ely ran the motor and jigged a yellow lead-head and minnow for walleyes.

They each looked their parts. Ely wore brown work pants and seasoned leather boots, a brown plaid shirt, and porkpie hat. Kristian did his hoping in a blue hooded sweatshirt, jeans, running shoes, and a camouflage Jones cap.

Kristian's rod was a stout Zebco that doubles for the shorecasting he does in Lake Superior. He isn't sure what kind of spinning reel he has.

"I don't know," he said. "Mistreely gave it to me."

Ely has given Kristian much of the tackle that fills his three-tiered box. The rest of it Kristian found or his father, Klaus, bought for him.

"You fishin' with a spinner?" Kristian asked the third person aboard.

"Yep," I replied.

"I don't like fishin' with those. I've lost about 2000 of 'em. That's why I'm fishin' for northerns."

Suddenly, he reared back on his rod.

"I got somethin'!" he said.

Ely looked up slowly.

"Oh, I lost it," Kristian said.

Ely has witnessed this scenario before.

"There are some weeds down there, Kristian," he said. "Maybe you had a weed."

They worked out of the bay, through the narrows and into a cove that led to the main lake. At 10:30, Ely slipped the four-horse into neutral and applied pressure to a hook full of fish. "Got something," he said. "Feels like a northern."

Kristian sprang for the landing net and hovered over the gunwale. Ely guided the hammer-handle northern up to the side of the boat. Kristian swooped. No problem. One northern in the boat.

Kristian dived into the hook-extraction process while Ely watched. Then Kristian held up the fish.

"Is this too small to keep, Mistreely?"

"I think so," Ely said. "What do you think?"

Kristian didn't bother to answer. He tossed the fish overboard and peered into the water to watch it swim off. Then he got back to fishing.

While he fished, he asked questions.

"How many pounds do you think that thing was, Mistreely?"

"Oh, maybe a pound or two," Ely replied. "You can make 'em grow as big as you want. We won't tell on you."

Other questions were more abstract.

"Do big walleyes eat little northerns?"

"How did you get to be an outdoors writer?"

"How come fish don't have that much blood?"

They were the kinds of things grown-up anglers probably wonder about, too, but just don't ask out loud, like the one Kristian asked a little later: "How come on those fishing programs, the people are always catching fish? As soon as they throw the line in, they catch a fish. How do they do that?" Yeah, Al Lindner. How do you do that?

But Kristian had some answers, too.

"A northern, when it strikes, can go up to 30 miles per hour."

"The fish are supposed to be near shore now."

"Did you hear what they said on the news? They said your fish will taste a lot better if you put 'em in a cooler instead of on a stringer."

At 11:30, Ely hooked another northern.

"Better get the net, boy," he said.

The team went into action. Ely reeled. Kristian pounced on the net. Ely reeled. Kristian swooped.

Bingo. Another half-pound of northern.

"He's catchin' what I want to catch," Kristian said.

Kristian went from the orange plug to a Silver Minnow spoon to a plain hook and live minnow. Ely rigged him up with a floating jig-head and a live minnow, the same outfit that was working for Ely.

Kristian just couldn't score.

Ely hooked northern No. 3

"This can't be!" Kristian said. "Something's wrong here."

Ely hooked northern No. 4.

"I wonder why I'm not catching any fish," Kristian said.

Ely hooked northern No. 5.

"This is the pits," Kristian said.

But he never took his line out of the water. And he never quit wanting to catch fish. And he cheerfully landed all seven of the northerns and the plump perch Ely caught.

One can learn a lot about his fishing partner on days when the fishing is slow.

At 2 p.m., the fishing buddies went back to the landing to drop off their companion. Ely would have been ready to go home, though he didn't say so. Kristian seemed to have had enough.

But when they were about half a cove from the boat launch site, Kristian turned to his older friend and said, "After we drop him off, can we go back out, Mistreely?"

Mistreely smiled. "Sure," he said.

Summer/

30 Days
Wandering Fever
Words Unspoken
Your Fire, My Fire
Soul Country
Campfire Girl
Coming Home

30 Days

The place is a mess. A tube of seam sealer is lying on the coffee table. Half-filled Duluth packs slump next to the dining room table. Maps with lots of blue on them carpet a corner of the livingroom floor.

The couple who live here don't apologize. They're getting ready to paddle around Ontario's Quetico Provincial Park for a month. They will leave in a week.

This is the kind of trip many of us dream about. Too many of our jaunts in the woods are carved out of too small chunks of summer. But these two—a writer and a teacher—have torn a whole month off the calendar and put it in their packsacks.

She's baking the bread. He's seam-sealing a pack. She's buying the crackers and peanut butter. He's checking on permits and customs fees.

Both of them are wallowing in the accumulation of gear that has made their home look like a campsite.

Stuff sacks litter the floor in bulges of orange and blue and tan. A saw and ax lie on the dining room rug next to a stack of paperback books. On the dining room table sits a box that holds a pound of M&Ms, two boxes of crackers, and a half-pound of peanut butter. Nearby is a plastic bag filled with 45 rolls of Kodachrome.

At least three lists are floating around in the kitchen and dining room. Several items already have been crossed off. Many more have not been.

A tent and its poles are neatly packaged in a stuff sack on the floor. So are two sleeping bags. Lying loose, strewn between the dining room and living room, are a daypack, a camera, extra lenses, an empty journal, the seam sealer, the maps, plastic bags and fishing reels. Atop a cedar chest is a pamphlet entitled, "Fishes of Quetico."

The woman wants to know if a half-pound of peanut butter seems about right for half the trip. The man is showing off three rolls of single-ply toilet paper that he says will save space in the packs.

These paddlers are doing it right. They've started planning and packing and preparing far enough ahead of time to forget several essentials—and then remember them before it's too late.

But beyond that, they're having fun. If you didn't know for sure, you might think they had already embarked on this trip. They're immersed. They're consumed. They're experiencing it right in their living room.

It isn't the novelty of canoeing. They've been paddling the canoe country for years in three-day and four-day and week-long get-aways. But they've become kids going to summer camp all over again, because a 30-day trip is something else.

How much toilet paper do you need for a month of trips to the biffy? How many lunch crackers will a half-pound of peanut butter cover? How much is the customs duty on $200 worth of grub? The couple are making their best guesses. Chances are they'll end up with too much peanut butter or too little toilet paper. But they'll get by. They'll have to.

Along with all the mini-decisions about food and fishing and flashlight batteries, they have probably both wondered if a trip of this scope is a once-in-a-lifetime adventure, if somehow, among the babies and business commitments and bad backs that life can deal out, they might never do this again.

But they'll have done it once. They'll have made their Big Trip, and that summer will always have an asterisk beside it in their memories.

Now they're thinking about none of that. They've got decisions to make—about peanut butter and paperbacks and packsacks.

Wandering Fever

> When I was very young and the urge to be someplace else was on me, I was assured by mature people that maturity would cure this itch. When years described me as mature, the remedy prescribed was middle age. In middle age I was assured that greater age would calm my fever and now that I am fifty-eight perhaps senility will do the job.
>
> Nothing has worked. Four hoarse blasts of a ship's whistle still raise the hair on my neck and set my feet to tapping. The sound of a jet, an engine warming up, even the clopping of shod hooves on pavement brings on the ancient shudder, the dry mouth and vacant eye, the hot palms and the churn of stomach high up under the rib cage...I fear the disease is incurable.
>
> —John Steinbeck, *Travels With Charley*

The train station at Gillam, Manitoba, looks as if it might have been there forever. It's a wooden building, creamy yellow, as long and low as the bush country that surrounds it.

On each end of the building, in black lettering on a white background, is the word GILLAM.

Inside, the waiting room is a cheery red and blue, though even the walls can't do much to brighten up the old wooden benches. When a train comes up from Thompson, 120 miles to the southwest, or down from Churchill, 200 miles to the north, the community's Cree Indians come running down to the station to see who's arriving.

One of the Canadian National Railway employees opens the overhead door to the freight room and rolls out a handcart loaded with a few suitcases. He hands the suitcases up to the man in the freight car in return for whatever must come off at this stop —a tricycle, a couple of duffel bags, maybe some boxes of fresh fruit for the Gillam Hotel's coffee shop.

Along one wall of the freight car, on summer runs of the CNR, it isn't unusual to see a couple of canoes and a heap of Duluth packs. Somewhere on one of the train's two passenger cars is a group of canoeists. They've run the Hayes, the Gods, the Seal, or some other Manitoba River that flows to Hudson Bay. Now they're heading home.

One August a few years ago eight of us were sprawled across the soft red seats of one of those cars. We'd been 21 days on the Gods, and we were letting the Muskeg Express—as the Churchill run is called—take us home.

When I think about that trip, I get a warm feeling inside. It wasn't just the canoeing or the train ride through the bush. It was that wonderful, free feeling of being on the move. Traveling, seeing new country, putting a new perspective on the world.

I have had the same feeling lying on the dock at Washington Harbor on Isle Royale in Lake Superior, my head resting against my backpack, waiting for the *Wenonah* to ferry me across Lake Superior.

I have felt it while riding a bicycle along the back roads of northeastern Minnesota, stopping at nondescript corner stores to refill a water bottle.

I've felt it while riding a bus down along the Caribbean coast of Mexico, talking with a woman from Sweden.

I felt it almost 20 years ago, heading for Colorado with my brother in a 1964 Buick and a good song on the radio.

It isn't all good times, being on the road. Inevitably a flight will be delayed, a connection will be missed, or something will break down. Those are the risks of traveling in new country, by unfamiliar modes of transportation, or where your language isn't the one in common use. But they're all worth it, at least to this traveler.

It has been a while now since I've been on the road. I can tell. I get itchy when I'm walking downtown and see loaded bicycles leaning against a restaurant front. I want to forget the trivial matters on my list of tasks and ride off.

I get a pang of envy when I see some travel-worn hiker striding up the road with a backpack, destined for trailheads unknown. I want to throw my gear together and walk with him.

I get a serious longing when I jog past the railroad tracks at noon and hear an Amtrak diesel hissing and rumbling at idle. I want to throw my pack aboard and settle into a passenger car headed anywhere.

A couple of weeks would be good. A month would be better.

There's so much country out there. So many fine people to meet. So much "nothing" to do.

Steinbeck's right. The disease is incurable.

Words Unspoken

He's getting older now. The lines have deepened around his eyes, and his cheeks are a little gaunt where they didn't used to be. Oh, he's not old yet. Getting older, yes, but not old.

It bothers me just a little, and not just because he's my dad. It's that, for some time now, I've wanted to say some things to him and haven't ever gotten around to it.

I've wanted to thank him for that day at the lake when we caught all those bluegills, and for all those vintage fall mornings when I should have been in Sunday school but was tagging along on a quail hunt instead.

I want to thank him for introducing me to the gunpowder sweetness of a spent shell, to the rich aroma of coffee rising from the thermos-jar cup, to the fragrant dust of dry grasses that turn to powder under bootsoles.

It's been a few years now since he's gone afield. I'm not sure why. He still has his guns, and I'll bet that old coat that's faded to the color of corn shucks in October is still hanging on a peg somewhere at home. Maybe it was the dog. He never did get out much after Chico died.

We watch the old films at Christmas, watch ourselves come out of the garage, and put our guns in the old Falcon station wagon. We watch the quail running in the thicket, watch another covey scooting across the road one at a time, watch each other walk in over Chico frozen on point.

It would be so natural after the films to just sit and talk about those days. The silence after the screen goes dark seems to invite it. But instead, one of us gets up and goes out for another log for the fire, or asks some trite question about the house or the car or the job.

I wonder how long I'll wait to let Dad know how much all that meant to me. I wonder why I haven't yet.

I suppose some guys are good at it, but I suppose a lot more of us sit with dads in deer shacks or duck blinds thinking about those days and not saying how we really feel.

Oh, we talk about the hunts and the fishing trips.

"Remember the day you had that big walleye on," you say, "and I knocked him off the hook with the net?"

Or, "Remember the time it snowed, and we shot the geese?"

We can talk about the days, all right, about the guns and the game and the gales, but that's where it stops.

Why is it so hard to look your Dad right in the eye and tell him how you feel, gut level? How you loved him for taking you along when your attention span was about as long as it takes a teal to disappear downwind. How surprised you were when he told you you could take your gun out alone for the first time. How much you wanted to cry when you knocked the walleye off his hook, and how you choked back the tears because he told you, "Big boys don't cry."

Maybe it's hard for us to say those things because we choked back a lot of feelings along with those boyhood tears we didn't shed in front of Dad—just the way Dad probably did with his dad.

Well, big boys do cry. And sometimes they cry hardest, I suspect, when they wait too long to say the things that need saying.

Your Fire, My Fire

The rain came out of the swollen clouds with a vengeance. It seemed as if the drops were being hurled down at us instead of just falling. It was the first day of a week-long canoe trip up north. It rained that way all day, so hard I was wet to my underwear beneath my borrowed rain gear.

We made camp that night on the point of an island in a jumble of blown-down spruce. I remember the camp, because somehow, with a good saw and a good ax and some persistence, we got a fire going.

I'll always recall that little fire hissing to life after several ill-fated attempts. We were green in the woods in those days, still learning the virtues of different kinds of wood and the little tricks of fire building, yet we made fire on an evening I didn't think a fire could be made.

Recalling the fires I've kindled on little spits of land across the North Country gives me a good feeling, like thinking of old friends I haven't seen for a while.

I remember staring into the fire one night at dusk when the moose walked up to our camp on Kahshahpiwi Lake.

I remember the fire we built on a chunk of granite one midday in the Quetico, when we needed to warm up after a September morning's paddle.

I remember the fire we sat around, sipping blackberry tea, as we listened to the roar of No Name Falls on Manitoba's Gods River one summer.

It seems a good portion of my time in the woods is spent hunkered, propped or slouched in the glow of a good fire. And it ought to be a good fire—not a raging, pep-rally bonfire, but a healthy, well-conceived fire that burns with the right attitude.

This brings us to the art of building a fire. Each person has his or her own style of fire construction. One's fire-building methods are akin to a toothbrush: they're very personal things that shouldn't be tampered with by others.

You want to build the fire? Fine. Build it tomorrow night or at breakfast. This one's mine.

I prefer the little cabin style, in which the twigs and small branches are stacked in a four-sided affair with some birchbark in the middle for tinder.

That's just my style. I have no qualms with your teepee style or the lean-to fire or some random configuration.

Now comes that critical, almost ceremonial, moment—the lighting. The Boy Scouts, among others, put a lot of stock in the one-match fire. I think it goes back to some survival instinct that has its roots in a Jack London story.

Usually the fire builder holds the match under the tinder until its flame is just about to nip his thumb. Then he drops the match, leans back, and assesses the situation.

If the small flames begin leaping and igniting the next-larger sticks, the fire builder is apt to think out loud something like, "Well, I think she's gonna go."

Though seemingly subtle, this remark is a bold commitment. It's the fire builder's signature. But the builder's job isn't finished. This isn't a communal fire yet.

The fire builder is also in charge of the second most critical period in the life of a young fire. It's time now for a few larger pieces of wood to be added, those about as thick as a lumberjack's thumb, or maybe the smallest of the pieces split by the wood gatherers. This is the adolescence of a campfire, that awkward stage between kindlinghood and full-stick maturation.

If the fire builder nurses his new flames through this touchy transition, the fire is officially a real fire. No mere statement serves to announce the fire's maturing to this point, however. The fire builder makes it official by walking away from the fire site, maybe to check the sunset or go pull his sleeping bag out of its stuff sack.

The walk is symbolic. It says, "OK, there it is. There's your fire. You can boil that water you wanted now or add another stick of wood whenever you feel like it. It's all yours."

Folks who are good in the woods know you don't mess with someone building a fire. Nothing is tackier than walking up to someone laboring with twigs and other forest tatter and saying, "No, no, no! Here, pile these like this." Not fair. Fires are personal things.

Nor does an honorable fire builder complain about the wood he was given to build a fire if the first few matches fail. A fire builder has the authority to reject fire-building materials before he uses them. He might want to replace those pine needles with some crisp, bare branches from the bottom of a spruce. He has the option to replace that punky birch with some good, dry cedar. But once the fire is built, it's his to take the glory or blame for.

Now we come to another art of the backcountry—fire tending. Fire tending is much different from fire building. First, it's not a solo job. It's a group affair. No matter where you're sitting around the fire, you're a fire tender.

Second, it's a free-lance undertaking. No Boy Scout Handbook has a chapter on fire tending. It's purely a matter of experience.

I was thinking about fire tending on a recent winter trip. The temperature was on its way to 20 below that evening, and we did a lot of fire tending.

Again, each camper has his or her own style. Some like to let the fire dwindle to that stage where it looks as if the coals are moving, then add a few more sticks. Others like to keep some fresh sticks on the fire almost all the time. Doesn't make much difference to me, though at 15 below I'd just as soon keep it stoked.

What does bug me, though, is when my fellow campers toss on a few new sticks of wood, each right next to the other. What that does is choke the fire, like putting a lid on top of it. A fire has to have air, and that means spaces between the logs about as wide as the logs themselves. At least that's how I see it. I hardly ever say anything about this, however. I just sit there, quietly dying with the fire, knowing how nice a fire it would be if it could just breathe.

Of course, the fire doesn't really die. It just sort of gags and smokes. This prompts the too-tight tender to take another stick and poke at the fire, or maybe get down on his knees and blow on its coals. But it doesn't solve the problem.

All that we plenty-of-air tenders can do is wait until it's time to throw on more wood, and make sure we do it—our way.

Meanwhile, a lot of minor tending is going on. In this category, you've got several moves. They include replacing a log that has rolled off the fire, scrunching the fire down so the logs are closer to the coals, correcting a leaning fire before it falls sideways, shoving unburned log ends into the main fire after the middle of the log has burned in two and removing an obviously punk piece of wood that insists on smoking. These are all important tasks, to be done by whoever is closest to what needs to be done.

This tending shouldn't be confused with diddling. Diddling is what you do with the fire that is non-essential and affects the fire only in an indirect way. Some examples of diddling are poking a long, thin stick into the fire to see if you can light the stick, using another stick of firewood to pull a single coal out of the fire to study it better, or pushing hot chocolate wrappers and other bits of waste farther into the coals where they'll burn more completely. Diddling doesn't amount to much, but it's fun.

Fact is, I kind of wish I were sitting out there now, under a well-strung tarp, in a light mist, staring into a nice bed of coals. It would be summer in my imagined scene, and a loon would be doing that lonesome wail in the next bay. I'd reach over and put a couple more sticks on the fire, allowing just the right amount of space between them, of course. Then I'd get down to some serious diddling.

Soul Country

The two stones are sitting on the stream bank. But then, they always are. They've come to be as much a part of this trip as the bratwursts at the A&W Drive-In in Iron River, Wisconsin, or the cigar pinched between Dave Zentner's teeth. The rocks, each the size of a grapefruit, are always left on the bank by Zentner and his fishing partner, Mark Kilen.

Zentner, fishing without Kilen today, sets each rock in his 17-foot canoe. They'll be used as anchors while Zentner flycasts. But not just yet. He has half an hour of poling up the stream to get where he wants to go.

The stream, which holds speckled and brown trout, flows cold and clear through northern Wisconsin, fed by numerous springs. Occasionally, it pauses along its way, becoming a small pond. It is one of these wide spots in the stream that Zentner is headed for this weekday afternoon.

He comes here often, a couple of times a week, all summer long—usually with Kilen, sometimes just with Duffy, the black Lab, always with a package of Dutch Masters Panatelas.

Zentner comes first for the fishing, for the brookies and browns he refers to as "marvelous lookin' animals." He always releases his catch. The barbs on the tiny hooks of his flies are pinched flat.

He isn't haughty about his fly fishing, as flyfishers often are made out to be—and sometimes are. He doesn't begrudge the worm and spinner anglers he sometimes meets on the stream. Zentner would simply rather not fish any other way than with flies. Part of it is the way a two-pound brown trout feels on the end of a two-ounce graphite fly rod. Part of it, too, is that Zentner believes flycasting is the most effective way to catch these trout.

But the trout—no matter how they're caught—are only part of this country's lure for Zentner. He's as apt to tell you about the waterfowl he sees while fishing, or the deer that snort in the blackness as he paddles back downstream at night.

"This is soul country," he says.

He is now poling through soul country toward a grassy point beneath some alders.

"I'm going to put you out up here," he says. "I want you to take a look at this spring."

There, in an opening in the trees, is a small pool, maybe six inches deep, four or five feet across and crystalline. Its bottom is sand, and it's moving. In several places, the sand is boiling where the spring bubbles up from the depths. It looks like Cream of Wheat being held at a simmer.

People stand around at Yellowstone National Park and click their Instamatics at less impressive hot pots. Yet here it is, quietly bubbling away in obscurity in the Wisconsin backwoods.

"Mark and I took turns lowering each other into that thing in our waders one day," Zentner says. "We never found the bottom."

On we go. Zentner points out stream improvements made by the Wisconsin Department of Natural Resources over the past several years. Channels have been narrowed, silt beds filled in with bough bundles.

The results of these projects swim by beneath us. The stream is alive with brook trout and brown trout in the six-inch class, shooting by like jet-powered shadows.

We pass the sharp bend where a kingfisher nearly took Kilen's hat off one evening. We pass the blueberry patch that has delayed more than one day's fishing. We pass the tailout where Zentner watched a black bear one night.

Then we are there.

The pond is perhaps a football field long and just as wide, surrounded by cattails and hummocks, with mats of floating weeds covering much of its surface.

"Somethin' risin' there," Zentner says from behind his cigar.

He's talking about the trout that are dimpling the water's surface along a reedy shoreline. He usually fishes the main body of the lake, but the action in this channel proves too enticing to pass up.

He shoots an arc of spit over the gunwale of the canoe and ties on a lighter tippet, the fine monofilament line to which he'll tie his fly.

It won't be an ideal day for flycasting. The wind is steady out of the southwest. Dark cumulus clouds are building on the horizon.

The stones are put into mesh bags and become anchors. Zentner strips some floating line off his fly reel and begins working the #12 Gold Rib Hare's Ear. If Zentner has tied it right, it will resemble an insect emerging from the stream bottom, rising to the surface.

He false-casts twice, then lays the fly on the water, letting it sink slowly. Nothing.

Again he presents the tiny morsel. Again, nothing.

A mature bald eagle appears over the ridge, soaring without effort. Like Zentner, it is fishing, but while the wind works against Zentner, it works with the eagle.

Zentner stops fishing and watches the bird, its head and tail a creamy white.

"Maybe they're starting to move," he says. "I usually don't see eagles around here until fall."

He watches the bird until it disappears, a period of a minute or so. The casts he misses in that time do not matter. This is soul country, and eagle watching is a part of it.

Again the Hare's Ear is moving. Now it's down.

Coming in, it snags some weeds. Zentner retrieves the fly to remove them.

"Even paradise has problems," he mutters.

Zentner looks something like a cross between a cowpoke and Tom Sawyer. He wears a denim shirt, bluejeans turned up at the bottom and hunting boots that have seen their share of duck blinds. His face is somewhere under a massive brown cowboy hat and behind a pair of polarizing sunglasses.

"I bought this hat in Rapid City, South Dakota," Zentner explains. "I used to laugh at guys in these things. Then I got caught out in a rainstorm, and figured out you could smoke a cigar in the rain under it."

Suddenly the end of his 9-foot fly rod is quivering, and a palm-sized brook trout is dancing in the water. It dances for just a few seconds, then is gone.

"Good. We don't have to traumatize him any more than we did," Zentner says.

We pull up the stones and move to another part of the pond. On our way we flush a dozen blue-winged teal and a couple of mallards. They make another pass over the cattails, low enough that we hear their wings slicing the autumn air.

"Ohhhhhhh," Zentner moans.

Soul country.

The thunderstorm that had been building on the horizon will pass to the north. The wind, however, continues to make casting difficult.

Afternoon becomes evening. A frog croaks. The Hare's Ear isn't fooling any more trout. But if Zentner is disappointed, he isn't letting on.

"I know it's been said a long time ago," he says, "but if you aren't going to catch fish, what better place to do it?"

He pulls up to his sitting rock on shore to have a Coke. He crosses his legs, clasps his hands around his knee and contemplates his pond world. He looks as comfortable as if he were in an easy chair.

The spring bubbles to life behind him, trickles down the shore and washes the gravel clean on its way into the pond. It is so cold, one's fingers begin aching in less than half a minute when held in the water.

Soon Zentner is back in the canoe, fishing again, saying the kinds of things anglers say when the fish aren't biting.

"He's a low-life trout," Zentner says of a riser that won't take his Hare's Ear. "He's got no class. This place is full of 'em."

A moment later he finds a trout with class. It smacks his fly and goes slightly crazy at the end of his line. It goes as crazy as a four-inch brown trout can go.

Zentner brings the fingerling in quickly and shakes the hook from its tiny jaw.

"He's a monster," Zentner jokes. "The only reason his mother wasn't with him is that she just tried to eat him."

Evening becomes dusk, and dusk becomes night. Zentner is now flycasting in the wind, in the dark. He switches from the Hare's Ear to an Arrowhead, and from the Arrowhead to a Trude.

He almost always fishes until after dark. That is when the big browns come alive. He has taken many in the two- to three-pound class over the 12 years he's been fishing here. He figures the largest brown he's taken here is a four-and-a-half-pounder.

Tonight will not be one of those nights. Occasionally, a fish leaps clear of the water and slaps the surface on reentry. But little else is rising.

"You ought to see it on some nights," Zentner says. "There are so many rises, it looks like it's raining."

The Trude fools a small brown. Then it fools something bigger. In the night Zentner can only feel the fish and hear it flopping. It flops like a big fish. Then—silence.

"Ohhhh," Zentner says. "He got off. That was a nice one, too. Like I always tell Kilen, I release 'em on the third jump."

Zentner inspects the Trude, then begins casting again. But too much wind and too few fish finally convince him it's time to paddle back down the stream.

He hesitates at the pond's tailout, contemplating one more cast. Even that seems futile, though, and soon we feel the gentle pull of the current beneath the canoe.

We navigate in total darkness. The only light is a strip of stars overhead, defined by alder boughs that overhang the river. Zentner has a flashlight, but he knows the stream too well to need it.

"We gotta stay to the far right here," he says, and later, "Have we passed that stump yet?"

At one point something off in the alders is snorting at us, short, quick exhalations of breath. A deer, maybe, or a bear.

Then we are pulling up to a bank on the left. It is smooth and grassy—our put-in point.

In the beam of the flashlight we repeat Zentner's going-home ritual. The canoe is emptied of rods, packs, boat cushions, and paddles. The canoe pole is wedged beneath a thwart and the stern seat, and tied up front to another thwart. Anchor ropes are stowed.

We load the gear in the car, tie on the canoe, and drive into the Wisconsin night.

Behind us, on the stream bank, sit the two stones.

Campfire Girl

At 57 she decided it was time she went camping. Oh, she'd been a Campfire Girl growing up in Nebraska. She'd spent most of seven summers as a camper or counselor at good ol' Camp Kiwanis on the Blue River. But that was mostly skits and songfests, cabins and cots. It was also 40 years ago.

Now she was twice a grandmother, and here she was lugging a 35-pound Duluth pack across a quarter-mile portage into the Boundary Waters Canoe Area Wilderness.

She looked more like she belonged on a tennis court at some swank Sun Belt resort. The floppy-brimmed golf hat she'd borrowed from her husband was emblazoned with the words "Valley Inn and Country Club."

Her white shorts and blue oxford-cloth blouse seemed far too clean to be on a canoe trip. The rocks and mud on the portage were quickly taking their toll on her Nike running shoes and Izod footies. But she wasn't kicking. She wanted to be here.

She had flown up from Missouri alone, leaving the restaurant business to her husband for a few days.

She had tried to talk a daughter and a couple of daughters-in-law into making the camping trip with her. She still chuckled, recalling their responses.

"That's nice. You should do that," her 27-year-old daughter had said.

"That sounds nice, but I don't think I'd care for it," said a daughter-in-law.

Then there was this matter of her husband. They had always made their trips together. She had never gone off on her own like this.

"How would I even get away from home? That was the first thing," she said. "Was it all right to leave my husband?

"'Are you really going to go through with this?' he asked me one time, like it was some big, horrible deal I was putting myself through. But then he accepted it real well. He realized I was going to do it. At the end, he was excited for me."

So the three of us headed into the backcountry east of Ely, Minnesota. Three lakes and two portages later, we made camp on a jutting piece of the Canadian Shield on Disappointment Lake. Already the magic of the Border Country had cast its spell.

"Look how clear that water is," she'd said when we'd launched the canoe.

Amazed that the lake water also was drinkable, she scooped up several handfuls as we paddled along.

On Disappointment, a great blue heron coasted past just off the bow of our canoe. We watched it make a soft landing on some rocks near an island, then begin walking that slow and cautious heron walk.

"Look," she said. "He walks like he's carrying a pack."

At camp, she was mesmerized by the gentle lapping of water on the rocks. More than once, standing in the middle of camp, looking out over the lake, she said in hushed whisper, "Listen to the water."

She sat in the sun. She napped on the rock. She helped gather wood, and she built the supper fire.

She admitted she'd had some concerns about her physical ability to make the trip. "I wondered if I could even canoe still, if I'd get too tired," she said.

She hadn't even counted on carrying a pack.

"I just thought, 'You mean I'm going to carry one of those packs, one of those huge things?' But I just thought of it as one step at a time. I just figured you had to do it," she said.

And she did.

"It wasn't easy, but I felt real good, like, 'Hey, I did it.' You also feel like you're part of the trip, not just coming along for the ride," she said.

That evening, the North Country put on one of its finest displays. The sun dripped over the far ridge and sent shafts of pink up through the clouds on the horizon. The lake was a piece of glass, and the loon calls echoed from ridge to ridge.

I'm not sure who had the best time, the one on her first camping trip or the ones who took her along into the country they love.

It isn't often a paddler gets to share the canoe country with one who appreciates it so much. It's even more special when she happens to be his mother.

Coming Home

The penny lay in the gutter next to a broken Dairy Queen spoon, some faded lawn clippings and pieces of brown glass. Bent under the weight of his Duluth pack, the man paused a moment to ponder the unlikely collection. He was coming home from a week in the woods. A week of paddling and portaging and sun and mosquitoes, a week of pure water and clear air and the sweet smell of duff on the forest floor. Now there was this junk in the gutter.

Welcome home.

As renewing as a week in the bush can be, this matter of coming back to the world we left behind is always a slap in the face. Like a space capsule returning to earth from its weightless odyssey, we need some kind of reentry shield to protect us in our reunion with civilization.

The process had begun when he was still paddling. Subtly, at first, the signals appeared: a cabin tucked up on the shore, people milling about on a dock, a boat tied up alongside. A bridge loomed across the river in the distance at the take-out point, its angular girders in stark contrast to the natural world with its softer shapes. A woman walked a dog at the water's edge. The dog yapped incessantly as the canoe passed by, shattering the silence that had accompanied the canoeist for a week. Even that paled when compared to the motorboat whining in big circles on the river, whipping a water skier around like coach twirling a whistle on his finger.

The paddler liked bridges and dogs and water skiing—no philosophical hang-ups there—but it had been so much nicer without them.

The trip ground to a halt as the bow of the canoe grated up against the gravel at the landing. Packs, paddles and canoes were loaded and lashed to the trailer. The cushioned seats of the van seemed foreign to rear ends more used to rocks, logs and canoe seats.

Two hours later the canoeist and his friends found themselves spilling out onto the main street of Two Harbors, Minnesota, for lunch. The bustle of North Shore traffic through the heart of town jolted the group to reality.

Duluth, where the paddler left his friends, was the same, but on a grander scale. The heavy beat of rock music from a stereo tape player drowned the roar of rapids in the Lester River where he unloaded his gear. Passing cars hissed by as they climbed the hill away from Lake Superior. There's nothing inherently wrong with rock music or the hum of a bustling city, but it had been so much nicer without them.

No one came to pick up the solitary canoeist and whisk him off to his home by car. He had planned it this way. He shouldered his pack, grabbed his fishing rod, and began the hour's trek up the hill toward home, past the penny and piece of spoon and dried grass clippings, past the toddler's tennis shoes on the curb and impatient cars at busy intersections, past the street construction and its swirling dust.

He tried to pretend it was just another portage, but the city wouldn't let him.

Fall/

Marking the Seasons
Forgotten Stand
Little Creatures
Brule by Night
Cabin Time
Northern Lights

Marking the Seasons

I pulled my vest off a peg in the back hallway. The dog already knew where we were going. He was standing with his nose at the crack of the back door, waiting. We do this almost every night, he and I. The late evening walk.

It was raining lightly on this September weeknight, so I threw a rainjacket over the vest. Then I clipped the rope to the dog's collar, announced our departure, and we were off.

I used to think we took this evening walk mostly for the dog's benefit. Now I've come to believe differently. I think I derive as much from the late evening walk as he does.

As much as my heart yearns for the woods, I am essentially an urban being. I don't like to admit it, but it's true. I spend a lot more time than I would prefer waiting at traffic lights, looking for parking places and sitting at a small desk in a large building. My world is climate-controlled, except for short hops from house to car and car to office.

I find myself looking forward to these nightly forays with the dog to reclaim my kinship with the natural world. Here is my chance to smell the air, feel the earth, and watch the sky.

The dog isn't interested in such lofty human pursuits, of course. He just wants to find out which neighborhood dogs have had the audacity to invade his territory since our last walk. He uses the late-night walk to reestablish the boundaries of his territory. He wasted no time. We had barely cleared our own driveway before he was anointing Frank and Susan's lilac bushes. From Frank and Susan's, it's down the alley behind Hoiviks' and onto the side street.

The rain was falling in a fine mist, the kind you don't see until you look up toward the streetlight at the corner. It was a cold mist, or at least it seemed that way after the warm rains of summer. But I wondered, if this same rain were falling in April or May, if it wouldn't seem like a warm rain.

While I was watching the mist materialize beneath the street-light, the dog was sniffing at the base of the light pole. This is a regular stop on our route, always worth a good 10 or 15 seconds of sniffing. I usually don't hurry him at such times. He doesn't hurry me when I've stopped to search for the North Star or Orion.

As usual, the light pole was far too substantial to pass up as a boundary marker. The leg went up. The mark was made.

The chill in the air and the wood smoke from a neighbor's chimney made me wonder how soon we'd be making this walk on snowpacked streets. I remembered all the walks when footsteps crunched and the air was so cold it burned the insides of my nostrils. I remembered looking up at streetlights and watching a sky full of snowflakes swirl to earth.

I also recalled the dirty, diminishing snowbanks and street full of sand. I remembered the first night last spring when I heard the peepers calling from the woods across the street. And I remembered the summer night when a barred owl was calling from somewhere down by the cemetery.

As the dog marks his territory, I mark the passing seasons.

The dog passed up a couple of his regular stops in our next

block. For some reason, he wasn't interested in the railroad ties at the house where the two Irish setters live or the driftwood lawnscape at the white house on the corner. He hit the streetlight at the end of the block, however, as was his custom. Then we moved into the dark mid-block area where bushes line both sides of the street.

It occurred to me that this is where I do most of my stargazing on our walks. Here the city lights are most obscured by bushes and trees, allowing the most undiluted view of the sky. Standing there, I often wonder how much clearer the stars would look from some campsite in the canoe country.

Tonight, though, was not a night for starwatching. It was a night for contemplating maple leaves rain-plastered to the pavement and bare tree branches against the clouds.

Then it was one more streetlight, a spruce tree at the gray bungalow, and on up the hill toward home. The yellow glow coming though the livingroom curtains looked warm and inviting. We paused at the back door so I could unsnap the dog's rope from his collar.

Inside, I hung up my rain jacket and vest, and wiped the mist from my glasses. It had been a short rendezvous with the natural world—short, but for an urban outdoorsman, satisfying.

Forgotten Stand

It's hard to say how long the deer stand has been there. Its wooden framework has been weathered to the color of a November sky. Its platform boards—the ones still remaining—are warped and loose. Even the aspens that support the stand are dead and wobbly. One is half gone. Still, like a leaning tree that refuses to fall, the stand hangs on. It sits there, soaking up sunshine on this October morning as it has for countless Octobers.

No hunter will sit upon the stand come deer season. The structure has long since lost its value as a usable platform, but it will be there, just the same. It will sway when the wind moves the aspen trees, just as it always has.

Whoever built the simple stand knew what he was doing. The ridge it's on is perhaps 20 feet higher than the surrounding countryside. It overlooks a small pothole a whitetail would walk down to for a drink.

Beyond the pothole, the country rises again. It's mostly aspens, with a few balsam firs.

The stand itself is simple. It consists of a couple of two-by-fours nailed between the two aspens, with a few flat pieces across the top for a platform. It's no wider than 18 inches at its broadest point, and perhaps six feet off the ground.

Halfway up to the stand, on one aspen, a small log has been nailed for a climbing step.

That's it.

On this October morning, the wind is coming out of the south, just the way you'd want it if you were hunting from the stand. Though lower in the sky than it was a couple of months ago, the sun is warm enough to make a nap inviting. One couldn't help but wonder if the hunter who used this stand had enjoyed such mornings himself.

And what other warm memories does this simple stand have to share?

Did it have a name at one time? Was it an X on some topographic map that hunters called the Pothole Stand? Or the Ridge Stand? Or maybe it simply carried the name of the hunter who built it—Rollie's Stand, or Dave's, or Tom's.

How many frosty mornings did someone sit here and curse the cold? How many candy bars were unwrapped in stealth on this platform? How many cigarettes were smoked in slow motion here? How many empty cartridge casings were ejected into the grass below? How many gray jays alighted in these aspens, cocking their heads and inspecting the lump of humanity sitting there? How many mornings did someone watch the sun rise from the cluster of white pines to the east? How many deerless days did someone watch the sun disappear over the balsams to the west?

How many times did these boards sense the muffled thumping of a young hunter's heartbeat as he watched a buck work its way out of the aspen and down to the water, pausing, flicking those big ears back and forth every few steps?

How many times did the hunter's bullet find its mark? How many times did it lodge harmlessly in the duff beyond?

And what of the hunter who once used this spot? Is he, like the boards themselves, older now, weathering gracefully with the years? Or has he gone the way of the aspens, his stand a memorial to some of his most pleasant hours on Earth?

Perhaps, during the coming deer season, a whitetail will meander through the aspen, nibbling twigs as it goes. It will stop in the clearing by the pothole, head up, ears perked. It will wait.

Soon, it will move on down to the water. The wind will be out of the south. For some reason, unknown to the deer, it will pause before drinking and look up the ridge. It will stand there, motionless, staring. Then it will drink, and disappear into the aspens again.

Little Creatures

The juncos have been moving through lately. You've probably seen them—small, gray birds with bars of white along the outside of their tailfeathers.

In the bird world, juncos are pretty much your average bird. They aren't nearly as striking as, say, a pileated woodpecker. They aren't as fun to watch as a kingfisher or an osprey. They don't have the busybody personality of a chickadee.

But each fall when they come through, I take note. I don't know where they're coming from, and I'm not sure where they're going. But, to me, they're as much a part of this time of year as bare aspen branches against a brooding sky or the feel of the swamp beneath my waders. My world is richer because of juncos.

It used to be that I looked at the bird world only through the eyes of a hunter. I knew quail and pheasants and grouse and geese. In short, the only birds I cared much about were those I could shoot at each fall.

There were game birds and—as we called them—tweety birds. A tweety bird was just something that caught your eye momentarily, something to be dismissed as soon as you realized it wasn't a game bird.

Somewhere along the way, not all that long ago, that began to change. I met a couple of people who knew a lot about birds and were willing to share that knowledge. Tweety birds became chickadees and red-breasted nuthatches and ruby-crowned kinglets and white-throated sparrows.

As I got to know them, certain ones came to be symbolic of the seasons. The days can begin to warm after a long winter, but until you've heard your first white-throated sparrow, it just isn't spring.

When I hear my first ruby-crowned kinglet each year, I am almost always on some point of land in the canoe country a few days after ice-out. We go to fish for lake trout, but the trip wouldn't be the same without the kinglet's warbling from the trees.

In the same way, nuthatches are lazy summer days under old pines, and juncos are bouncing drives along gravel roads in a truck loaded with duck decoys.

And it isn't just the birds. It's muskrats and field mice and mink droppings. It's mayflies and midges and mushrooms. All of them, in some way, have become part of the fabric of a season or a pursuit. Muskrat huts are mornings on the marsh. Field mice are corn rows that cackle with pheasants. Mayflies and midges are fat rainbow trout dimpling the surface of a backcountry lake.

I don't think I'm alone in this. I have seen a trout angler wistfully look out of his office window and bet aloud that a green drake hatch was happening on his river that afternoon.

I know of a deer hunter who likes to put his stand higher than most others in an aspen tree. He does it so he can watch the warbler migration when the deer aren't moving.

I have ice-fished with a brook trout fisherman who could tell you whether the woodpecker drumming nearby was a downy or a hairy by the way its tapping tapered off.

Lately, I've been wondering just what it is about all these little awarenesses that makes our hunting and fishing richer. It isn't that they help us catch more fish or shoot more birds. It's something completely apart from that.

I don't believe it's just a matter of ego, a way to impress one's fellow hunters or anglers with knowledge of the natural world. It's deeper than that. For me at least, it is a matter of putting things in perspective. When you recognize the inherent value of all creatures, you begin to look at the whole world a bit differently.

I have sat while deer hunting and watched a red beetle spend 20 minutes crawling out from under a leaf and across a patch of dirt I'd scraped with my boot heel. I have stood in a duck camp and watched a bald eagle soaring effortlessly across the heavens. Both creatures are equally important parts of the natural world. Both served to enrich a hunting experience. Both made me contemplate my own place and time here on Earth.

That, I suppose, is the root of all this. Sooner or later, while considering the juncos and the muskrat lodges and the beetles, you come to consider your own niche in life. And when you've done that, the trout in your hand or the buck at your feet is all the sweeter.

Brule by Night

Steve Therrien's fly line laced the night air over Wisconsin's Brule River.

Whiss-whiss.

Whiss-whiss.

Whiss-whiss.

Whissssss.

Somewhere in the blackness, below the silhouette of some cedars, the fly came to rest. It was an Angleton, an imitation designed to entice the Brule's big brown trout.

"It looks like somebody took a mouse, hit it with a hammer, and then put wings on it," Therrien said. "It throws a nice wake, and it's small."

Therrien was throwing the Angleton from the bow of an 18-foot Grumman canoe. In the stern, David Spencer knelt on a boat cushion and held the canoe in position with two snubbing poles.

The poles were each six feet long and about two inches thick. One was made of spruce, the other of pine. Spencer held the poles against the river bottom and braced their upper ends against his forearms and biceps. He looked like a man on crude crutches. His eyes scanned the river.

"You got a rise at 11, about 20 feet downstream," he told Therrien.

Therrien knew at once that Spencer meant a brown trout was rising to feed just to the left of the canoe's bow downstream. Therrien lifted his fly off the water and began false-casting.

Spencer watched the line working.

"A little more downstream," he said.

Therrien made the correction.

"There you go," Spencer said. Therrien made two more false casts and let the Angleton descend again. He stripped line in slowly, steadily, letting the fly make its wake.

If there were a brown trout swimming there, it was too smart to fall for a mouse that looked as if it had been smashed by a hammer.

Spencer lifted the snubbing poles and let his canoe—"the old river barge"—move downstream. He and Therrien had done this hundreds of times, but rarely in the same canoe. They are Brule River guides, among the youngest of the clan who have chosen to carry on an old way of life on the river.

"There's a really rich tradition of guiding on this river," Spencer said. "We try to keep that going by showing people a different way of being in the woods, to enjoy simply being here, not having to catch fish to enjoy being out."

Spencer and Therrien have been guiding since the mid-'70s. Spencer spent most of his childhood summers at his parents' cabin on the river. He has had a pair of snubbing poles in his sinewy arms since he was seven or eight.

Therrien came into guiding through the back door. "I got roped into it," he said. "Spencer asked me if I wanted to guide one night. Hell, I didn't know he meant run the river at night with the rapids. But I didn't wreck the boat. I figured if I did it once, I could do it again."

Most of the two men's guiding is done for the well-heeled cabin owners of the upper Brule, or for those cabin dwellers' well-heeled friends. They are fly fishers from Minneapolis, Milwaukee, Chicago, Boston, Duluth, or Washington, D.C. They pay Spencer or Therrien $50 to $80 for a night on the river, but, as Spencer said, they are paying for more than just the fishing.

They come for the steaks and hash browns and corn on the cob and red wine and black coffee the guides prepare on the shore of the Brule. And they come simply to experience night on the river.

On this September evening we had put in at Stone's Bridge at about 6 p.m. Spencer had paddled downstream a mile or so while Therrien threw a Rat-faced McDougall to uninterested trout. Foregoing the classic dinner, we had eaten sack-lunch suppers near a streamside spring and waited for darkness.

Then we had reloaded the canoe by flashlight and pushed off. It would be a cold night to sit in an aluminum canoe on 55-degree water.

"When you can see your breath at dusk, you know it's going to be a cool night," Spencer had said.

By now, Spencer was wearing polypropylene long underwear, wool pants, a wool shirt, a wool sweater and a Peruvian stocking cap with earflaps. Therrien also wore polypropylene, along with a blue chamois shirt, khaki pants, an Alaskan wool shirt, a buffalo-plaid wool shirt, and a navy-blue stocking cap.

Therrien isn't petite in the first place, at 6-1 and 200 pounds. Sitting there in the bow, layered in his wool, moving only his right arm, he resembled a tombstone someone had thrown a jacket over.

The river was alive with night sounds. A barred owl hooted his "Who cooks for you? Who cooks for you all?" Bats twittered overhead. Water gurgled along the keel of the old river barge. Occasionally, we would hear deer sloshing along the stream banks.

"I think you really learn to appreciate the fullness of things," Spencer said, trying to describe the essence of nighttime on the Brule. "There's a whole lot more going on out here than most people ever see."

Fullness. The word seemed to fit. Perhaps it is because, at night, you use more of your senses to experience the river. You feel the subtle movements of the canoe as it slides across a patch of watercress. You hear Spencer's calloused hands as they slide along the snubbing poles. You smell the earthy pungence of night air.

"This is the fall smell," Therrien said. "In spring it's a lot sweeter, real organic. In summer it's sort of a warm sweet."

In fall it's a boggy, dusky smell—full-bodied and rooty.

The canoe drifted through the pungence, cool air seasoning our nostrils. Therrien began working off the right side of the canoe. He was pointing his nine-foot graphite rod toward the stars, stripping the orange fly line through the guides, creating an invisible V with the Angleton. Suddenly, he rocked his tombstone torso back and lifted his rod high. At once the sound of splashing came from near the bank in the darkness.

"There's a fish," Therrien said.

He said it in a calm, satisfied way that seemed to fit the evening's mood. Spencer held the canoe steady with the snubbing poles and somehow readied the landing net. The splashing came closer and closer, until we could see the fish alongside the canoe. The fish was a brown trout, about 11 inches long. Spencer removed the fly from the fish's jaw and let the trout swim out of the net. Spencer shook the net out and replaced it in the canoe.

He and Therrien were not on the Brule to fill their freezers with 11-inch brown trout—or any size browns, for that matter. The guides don't keep many fish, and they speak with disgust of the "Jitterbuggers" who night fish the Brule with their treble-hooked Jitterbug lures and keep the five browns that regulations permit.

"Five of those fish a day is too many," Spencer said. "Two of those big fish is too many."

We moved downstream, fishing pools and runs whose names are older than any of us in the canoe: Buckhorn Spring, the Outflow, the Dining Room Pool.

Therrien and Spencer traded places, Spencer fishing now, Therrien snubbing.

Owls called. Stars fell. A dog barked. Somewhere near the top of the Dining Room Pool, a fish rolled. No one saw it, or even the ripples from it, but clearly, from the substantial sound of it, here was a fish to be reckoned with.

"Yeah," Spencer said. "There we go."

"That," Therrien said, "is a nice fish."

Spencer started working the unseen fish with a Hank's Creation, a cork-bodied fly that looks something like a thimble with tailfeathers. The fly's cork body is painted silver. Eyes of red and yellow are painted on its front end. From under the wrapping of black thread, along the side of the body, come sprigs of mallard feathers, dyed goose quill and dyed goat tail. The body has a deer-hair tail that covers the shank of the fly's #2 hook.

Therrien tied five-and-a-half dozen Hank's Creations last winter. One of them was on the end of Spencer's leader now.

"That was a nice fish," Spencer said, two fruitless casts later.

"He had some girth to him," Therrien said.

This was one of the moments Spencer had been talking about earlier. The Brule is home to some big browns. When one of them is feeding, and your Hank's Creation is throwing a nice wake, and the stars are reflecting in the river, it's about all a fly fisher can stand. Or, as Spencer had put it: "When you're fishin' in the front and a big fish starts floppin' and it sounds like God's throwin' bricks, your heart gets pumpin'."

Spencer's must have been pumpin' as he worked the Hank's across the pool. Several times, Spencer lifted his fly off the water and put it down again, but the fish wasn't to be fooled.

Finally, reluctantly, Spencer told Therrien to let the canoe drift on downstream.

In the Willow Pool, just below a wing dam's riffle, Spencer caught and Therrien released another small brown.

"Fishing on the river has really gone down a lot in the last 30 years," Spencer said. "Many of the old guides won't even take people out unless they're friends. I tell my people, 'We might not catch fish.' Every time they get a strike they should be happy."

A nice Brule brown is an 18-inch fish, perhaps a two-pounder.

"Most people would say you have a real nice fish if you get a four-pounder," Spencer said.

The biggest brown Spencer or Therrien had heard of in the last couple of years was an eight-pounder.

Sometime after 10:30 p.m. the two guides changed places again. We drifted past more cedars and white pines, through the Green Bridge Hole, past Sally's Cabin and down Hungry Run. Then, after a bulging of the river, it narrowed and tumbled through a run of frothy water called The Falls. It wasn't truly a falls, and it was primarily a straight shot with standing waves, under some low-hanging cedars. But it was dark and loud.

"At The Falls, you always feel like you're dropping into the gates of hell," Spencer said.

He sculled with a paddle to align the canoe at the lip of the falls. Satisfied, he stroked hard and the Grumman dropped into the fast water. Trees materialized over our heads and were gone before we could have reacted.

At the bottom, where the river cranks hard to the left, Therrien reached out for a couple of draw strokes. The canoe went gliding out into a wide pool of quiet water. The experience was something like being born.

A few minutes later an albino mouse went scooting across the water, and a 17-inch brown slurped it down. Fortunately for Therrien—unfortunately for the brown—the mouse was an imitation tied to a hook on the end of Therrien's leader.

The fish thrashed and danced its way into Spencer's waiting net. Therrien shined his flashlight on the fish. It was a tawny brown, speckled with red and brown spots. Its eyes searched the suddenly bright night for something familiar.

"Want to keep it?" Therrien asked.

"Whatever you think," Spencer replied.

"Maybe one for winter," Therrien said.

Spencer pulled a small black stick, perhaps an inch thick and 18 inches long, from his pack. Therrien had one along, too. Priests, the anglers called them. "Because they deliver the last rites," Therrien said.

Spencer wielded the priest quickly and efficiently. He left the trout on the cold bottom of the canoe.

We had seen two boatloads of Jitterbuggers, three more whitetails and no more brown trout when we pulled up alongside the Spencer family cabin at midnight. We crawled stiff-kneed from the old river barge up onto the dock.

Rat-faced McDougalls, Hank's Creations, and albino mice. The Dining Room Pool, the Willow Pool, Hungry Run. Barred owls, whitetails, and the aroma of fall. Spencer was right about the Brule at night. It wasn't just the fish. It was the fullness.

Cabin Time

It is evening, and the hunters have returned. They have spent all day shuffling through six inches of South Dakota snow trying to put up a few pheasants. They hunted all the familiar covers, whose names stir memories of bygone hunts: Jake the Drake, Mallard Point and Lost Limit Slough. Now they are back.

Guns lean against cabin walls outside the bunk rooms. Felt-lined pac boots sit just inside the cabin door, clumps of snow in their laces turning slowly to water. The hunters mill about aimlessly, shedding vests, reorganizing shells, and laying gloves out to dry.

It is one thing to have a good hunt and go home. It is quite another to have a good hunt and go back to the cabin.

Here you don't worry about tracking in, or about a pheasant feather that ends up on the couch. Nobody is telling you what time supper will be ready and to get cleaned up. You're on cabin time now—and there's always plenty of cabin time.

John Quaintance, the hunter who owns this place, calls it a cabin, though it's more of a home. It has three bunk rooms, two bathrooms, a sliding glass door to the patio, and—we might as well admit it—a color television in the corner of the living room.

But a cabin is as much attitude as it is appointments, and this place has the right attitude.

An empty Skoal tin sits on the table. The groceries we brought in the day before are still mostly in their sacks on the kitchen counter. The dark liquid in a beer bottle nearby is not beer, but a lumpy mixture of previously chewed Red Man tobacco. One is careful when he reaches for a beer at this cabin.

The aroma is that of roast beef and onions, which have been simmering in the slow cooker while the hunters shot pheasants. But that will wait. The hunters have dogs to feed and birds to clean.

The Labs stand around, four tails wagging, as their masters dish out Gaines Burgers and Ken-L Ration. Most of them are accustomed to dry dog food, buy they won't always eat it after they've hunted hard, and they've hunted hard today.

The dogs slug down their food, then amble over to another dog's dish just to make sure she hasn't missed anything. She hasn't. Then the four of them are sprawled out on the floor, licking their feet and otherwise tending the minor ailments brought on by the day's romp.

Someone stokes the woodstove, and, two by two, boots and liners gather to warm themselves around the hearth. Hunting pants and long underwear are hung from doors to dry. Wool shirts and sweaters are draped on the woodpile near the stove.

Now the place is starting to smell like a cabin.

Add the sweet pungence of some Hoppe's No. 9 gun-cleaning solvent and the atmosphere is complete. Gunbarrels are swabbed, and chambers are sprayed with WD-40 for the following day's hunt.

The hunters slip into dry socks and bluejeans. Someone washes an armload of potatoes, and someone else cuts them up. They're thrown into a pot of boiling water. By the time the birds are cleaned, the potatoes will be ready.

Meanwhile someone has spread papers on the floor by the table, and the birds are laid out for cleaning. It's a ceremonial thing, this cleaning of birds. The hunters kneel around the papers facing each other. Each bird is inspected and assessed during the cleaning process.

"Geez, this is a nice, big bird."

"Look at all the fat on this one."

"Ooh, this must be the one that both of us shot."

Chances are, one of the dogs will get up and walk over sleepy-eyed to nose a cold bird. Just checking to make sure there's nothing left that needs retrieving. Satisfied, she'll return to lie down again. No matter that a feather is stuck to her nose. All the better for a hunting dog's dreams.

As the birds are cleaned, the day's hunt is relived. Several of the birds are shot again, and retrieved again.

After dinner the evening fades fast. Hunters are soon strung out on couches or draped sidesaddle over armchairs. One might even curl up with his dog on the floor to talk about the day's hunt over a good belly rub.

The hunt is digested one more time, this version over a drawn out whiskey and soda. Then someone damps down the stove, someone turns the boot liners so they'll dry on the other side and someone else lets the dogs out for a quick run. Then they all trundle off to bed.

Northern Lights

I don't know what makes the northern lights. I remember reading the scientific explanation somewhere along the way. I just don't remember what it said, and I'm not so sure I want to know anyway. I prefer to think of them as magic—or part magic, part Robert Service, and part Jack London.

I remember one summer night's display in the North Woods. Lordy, what a show—great misty-green shafts shooting out of the northern horizon, like a battery of search lights run by a madman, or a Fourth of July fountain you thought was spent, but suddenly sends two or three more bursts of light into the night. Then, suddenly, it wasn't just the northern horizon. It was all over, and all the way to the top of the sky—if such a place exists—as if the Earth were merely a baseball game, and the sky some pulsating domed enclosure.

When the lights are cooking like that, it's impossible to watch them long while standing up. You must lie down, on a back porch, a boat dock, a grassy pasture. That's the only way you can see the whole show.

That's what I was doing when they began to whirl and swirl

and snake across the sky. There a horizontal lightning bolt. Now a fluorescent serpent. Then a rippling from one horizon to the other.

Don't bog me down with talk of protons and ions. This is mystical, magical stuff. I can handle neutrons and electrons and positives and negatives in a laboratory. I can deal with them in the context of a nuclear power plant. But the sky? The whole sky lit up like this? Forget the facts. I'd rather dream.

I'm mushing my way over the Dawson Trail...I'm building the fire that will save my life...I'm alone in a lonely land, missing the one I love.

I can easily remember the first time I saw the lights put on a display of spellbinding intensity. We had gone to the Baptism River on the North Shore of Lake Superior one night to harvest smelt. The smelt weren't running, so we left the river, climbed a bluff overlooking the lake, and rolled out our bags under the stars.

We cooked fried chicken over a fire, then laid back to enjoy the night. It was then we saw that the sky was alive and shimmering with the green glow. Lake Superior, riled by an east wind, was crashing ashore at the foot of the bluff. At first we spoke often, ooh-ing and ahh-ing, eager to make sure each other had seen a particular burst or shape in the sky. Then for long periods we would say nothing, just lie on our backs, watching above and listening below.

Finally we went to sleep, but I remember waking several times in the night to see the light still cavorting in the sky. It seemed as if the lights worked their magic all night, though it might have been only for awhile. When I awoke again dawn was breaking over the lake. I've felt differently about this country from that morning on.

I'll admit that every time I see the lights, I wonder all over again what makes them happen, but that's where I leave it. Some things are better with the wonder left in them.

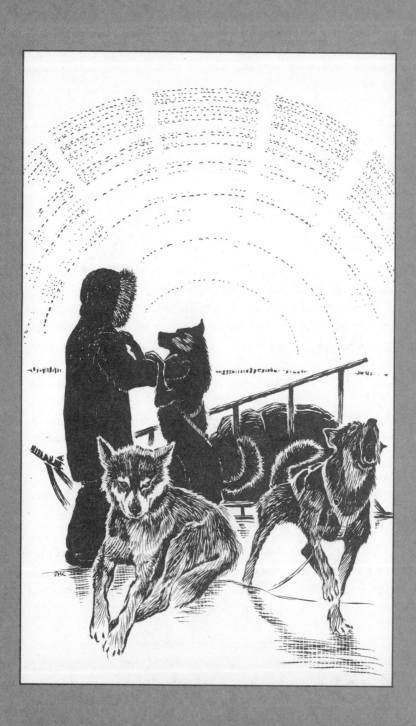

Winter/

Birkie Blues
A Season to Endure
In Stitches
Find the Magic

Birkie Blues

Number 262 shuffles his skis back and forth on the sugary snow. He isn't nervous. Heck, this is his third American Birkebeiner. Excited, yes. Nervous, no. He can't help it. He always gets this way at the starting line. Something about the music playing and all those skinny people in their skin-tight suits.

Quite a spectacle, this Birkebeiner, the 55-kilometer cross-country ski race held annually in the woods of northern Wisconsin between Hayward and Cable.

But it's so much more than a spectacle. It's a 34-mile journey into one's soul. This year, it's only a 31-mile soul search. The course has been shortened to avoid bad ice on Lake Hayward, near the start of the race.

The journey begins ominously for #262. When the cannon sounds to start the masses moving, one of his ski-pole baskets gets caught under another skier's ski. He goes down.

The Birkie is impressive enough when one is standing among 7000 skiers. It is even more moving when he is lying down, watching a good share of the 14,000 skis, 14,000 poles, and 14,000 legs go by.

Somehow, he is on his feet again, counting his blessings. Broken poles and broken skis are a way of life in this race.

Now #262 has some time to make up. He scoots along, picking off skiers. "Give me some room," he's thinking. "Let me ski."

Skiers are six and eight abreast here, each in his or her machine-set tracks. Like a Mercedes in Los Angeles rush-hour traffic, #262 weaves from lane to lane, looking for room.

Eight kilometers. Five miles. Feeling good. Legs are strong. Heart a-pumping. Lungs dishing out oxygen in liberal portions. This is no surprise. Things are always good at eight kilometers.

At 14 kilometers, #262 passes a man using one ski pole and one sapling from the woods, but he's making it.

Twenty-four kilometers. Fifteen miles. This is the finish line for the racers who are competing in the Kortelopet, the Birkebeiner's little sister.

Shortly after that, #262 cruises into one of several food stations along the route. He grabs a cup of Gatorade from a Cub Scout and slugs it down. The quick-energy drink is warmed. It goes down well. Then a cup of water to rinse away the fruity taste of the Gatorade, and an orange segment, just for fun. He passes up the powdered-sugar doughnuts.

Halfway, #262 is still strong—not blowing by people, understand, but strong.

He begins to think about times and rivals. He would like to improve on last year's 3:20 showing, maybe nip a couple of his friends.

Thirty kilometers. Eighteen-plus miles. Something's happening here, something ugly. These Wisconsin hills are no longer fun. Those 18-inch strips of purple klister ski wax—thicker than warm grape jelly, but thinner than grape Bubble Yum—aren't doing the job anymore.

More and more often, #262's skis go shooting out from under him, like a sprinter with no starting blocks. Each slip saps critical energy reserves.

But he bludgeons on. Is he skiing or shuffling? He thinks he knows the answer. He thinks those skiers moving past him know too.

Thirty-three kilometers. Another food station. Number 262 coasts through the crumpled paper cups and orange rinds to the side of the trail. He flips his skis off and looks at the bottoms.

His klister has worn almost completely off the inside of his skis. He tries a trick that worked last year, switching skis from one foot to the other. This puts the remaining wax on the inside edges again.

A cup of Gatorade. A cup of water. Half a doughnut. An orange quarter. On the road again.

He remembers other races, when that shot of Gatorade resulted in a surge of newfound energy. Where is that blast? Where has the go gone?

This is where the Birkebeiner gets mean. A series of hills culminates in the race's high point near the Seeley Fire Tower Hill at 37 kilometers (23 miles).

It might be the high point for the course, but it's the low point for #262. He is flailing now. No more thoughts of times and rivals. This is survival.

He fights it no longer. Atop the 37-kilometer hill, he pulls off the trail and kicks off his skis. He pulls a tube of klister from his fanny pack and squeezes long beads of it onto the bottom of his skis. He knows he's wasted now. His arm trembles as he tries to squeeze the high-viscosity wax from the tube.

But it works. He has purchase again. If only he could squeeze something like that into his veins. His legs feel like birch stumps in the woods, rotted from the rain. His arms feel like noodles.

He isn't sure he can finish. He is crawling now. Skiers whoosh past him. He feels as if he's a broken float in a parade.

He's paying now, paying for all the skiing he hasn't done in the past three weeks, three weeks that seemed too much like spring to him. He couldn't get his head into skiing. Now he can't get his arms and legs into it. He should have known. You can't bluff the Birkie.

Quit? Number 262 considers it. But there is no place to go. Practically speaking, he could probably get to the finish sooner by slugging it out on the trail—if he can get to the finish at all.

He thinks about all of this as the parade passes by. Old men, young women—perhaps a hundred in the last ten kilometers have passed him. Or 200. He doesn't care. None of that matters. What matters is the next stride, and staying on his feet through every icy downhill.

Forty-three kilometers. Twenty-seven miles. The race's last food stop appears ahead. It is like a calm cove on a windswept lake. Here is comfort, safety, and food. He quaffs a cup of Gatorade. He eats two doughnuts. More Gatorade. A swish of water. An orange slice.

Time doesn't matter. He watches the other skiers rush through, tossing down a cup of liquid and hurrying off. He remembers races like that. He knows how tired they are. But it's a good tired, full of accomplishment and aspiration. Nothing like what he's feeling now. Let them go, he thinks. Let them have their day.

Reluctantly, he shoves one ski forward, then the other. Mercifully, the course begins to descend again. Not that it's an easy coast, but at least the downhills begin to outnumber the uphills.

He thinks he will make it now. It won't be pretty, but it's possible.

Finally, #262 emerges from the woods. He hears the crowds, the announcer's voice baritoning through the Saturday afternoon.

Three hours and 23 minutes after he was lying among all those legs and poles and skis, it is over.

His time is not so much slower than last year's. It's just that he didn't have nearly such a good time making that time this year, and he had wanted to do so much better.

Funny thing, though. He feels the way he's felt at the end of every Birkebeiner before: the rush of emotion, the watery eyes, the quivery chin.

Why? What is it about this race that does that?

Number 262 knows. He isn't sure he can explain it, but he knows. It's that trip into his soul, into that little-known country we so rarely get to explore.

You can't do it sitting at a football game or sitting on a deer stand or watching the sun set over the lake. All of those things can be moving. All of them can stir a range of emotions. But something about an event of the Birkie's proportions reaches beyond all of that. Far beyond it, into the realm of risk and pain and triumph.

Number 262 didn't have the kind of day he might have had, not even the kind of day he's had before. But he probably learned more than he's learned at any Birkie past. He'll be back next year to find out.

A Season to Endure

We were skiing down a backcountry creek when we saw a dark spot poking through the ice and snow. This was four or five years ago, but the day stands out among all others I have spent on skis.

We stopped for a moment, waiting to see if the spot moved. It didn't. We skied closer and took a look. It was an elongated hump, maybe five feet long and six or eight inches at its high point, lumpy here and there, covered with dark fur. It didn't take us long to figure out that it was the top of a cow moose, the rest of which was beneath the ice. All that was protruding was the top of her head. Her ears had been gnawed off, probably by the wolves whose tracks were numerous in the snow surrounding the animal. That was all the wolves had been able to get at, though, and they had no doubt moved on in search of moose still on the hoof.

We stood there on our skis for quite a while, trying to piece together the events that had led to the moose's icy death. The ice in a large oval area surrounding the moose was about three inches lower than the ice across the rest of the creek. From the dirty and rough-crystalled edge of the exposed surface where the two layers of ice met, it looked as if the moose had broken through and churned up the water and mud in her struggle to get out again.

Finally, too weak to continue the fight, she had succumbed to the cold. The creek refroze around the animal, preserving her in her present state.

The creek was only about 25 feet wide at that point, and the animal was frozen less than a ski's length from one shore. Close, but a lifetime away.

We stood there for a long time, looking at what we could see of the moose, touching her fur, wondering.

We would never know for sure what happened, of course. Had the moose been sick? Had she been weakened in a long chase by wolves? Had a calf survived, being light enough to cross the creek without breaking through? Had it stood on the bank and watched its mother struggle until silent? Had it stayed there, waiting, wondering why she did not come ahead? Then, vulnerable and confused, had it become the wolves' next meal? Questions without answers.

We all like to think of the wilderness and its wildlife in neat, happy terms. The majestic bull moose, stripping leaves off a young aspen. Timber wolves howling from across the lake on a moonlit night. A beaver returning to its lodge at twilight, a freshly pruned branch between its teeth.

Too many storybook stories, where everything lives happily ever after. Too many Smokey the Bear posters where the birds and the beasts will have it made if only we aren't careless with matches.

Kids' books where the wolf kills the fawn don't sell. Nor, I suspect, would one in which mama moose dies an ugly, prolonged death by ice.

But sometimes life in the woods isn't pretty. The good guys don't always win. Nature can be cruel.

Another North Country winter is now upon us. We will make our safe little ski and snowmobile trips. We will take our pictures of snow-laden pine boughs and cheery chickadees.

For many creatures, though, winter is not a postcard scene. It is a season to endure, a matter of survival. It's been that way for centuries, of course, but it still smacks us in the face when we stumble across it.

In Stitches

The frumpy old booties sag against one another in a corner of the closet. Once their ripstop nylon shells were orange and bright. Now they are smudged and torn. Once their goose-down filling was full of puff and bounce. Now it's droopy and matted. They should have been chucked long ago, I suppose. But to understand why they haven't been, you have to go back to the Christmas of 1974.

When the booties arrived in the cardboard box, they weren't booties at all. They were a few pieces of ripstop nylon, some clumps of goose down sealed in plastic, a couple of knit cuffs and a sheet of instructions. The box had come from one of those sew-it-yourself kit companies. To a guy who didn't know his bobbin from his zigzag. But I was excited. I was going to make my wife a pair of booties for Christmas.

I had time, plenty of time. I started in November.

I had moral support. A couple of women at work and the wife of a friend said they'd give me any tips I needed.

What I didn't have was skill. I found out fast that I wasn't a seamstress—or seamster—whatever you call it.

I set up a card table in an extra room, shut the door to keep Phyllis—the intended receiver—at bay, got out all my booty ingredients, and uncased the sewing machine. From the very beginning, that machine was The Enemy. And this was supposed to be a decent machine. Lord knows, Phyllis could run it. She could make that thing hum. She made herself all kinds of clothes that looked just like store-bought.

Throughout the ordeal Phyllis knew I was making her something, of course. So she'd stand outside the door and try to guess what it was. I'd sit inside answering, "No...no...no...How do you thread a bobbin?"

Like the tower talking to a pilot in an emergency, Phyllis tried to talk me through it from the other side of the door. When I realized it was useless, I put away my booty stuff and let her come in. We got the bobbin threaded.

Out with booty stuff again, on with the project. First, you singe the edges of the nylon with a candle flame to keep them from fraying, the instructions said.

"What's on fire in there?" the voice outside the door would say.

"Hey, get outa here!" I'd say. "Did Betsy Ross have to put up with this?"

Giggles.

Eventually I got the fabric singed.

Then we got down to the needlework. That's when The Enemy got vicious. It would miss stitches. It would refuse to penetrate a glob of material. Or it would run amok, like a car with its accelerator pedal stuck.

I broke needles. I broke out in a sweat. I said bad words.

It wasn't all my fault. If ever a machine was made that was sexist, it was a sewing machine. They're built for slim little woman fingers with nice, pointy fingernails. Ever try to run one with pudgy little boy digits and smushed, bitten nails? Hopeless.

Each night I'd come home, eat supper, and report to my cell. I hated those booties. I hated that machine. Finally, I could stand it no more. I boxed up my booty stuff, cased up The Enemy and drove directly to the sewing machine store. I told the man what I was up to. I told him my problems.

"Hmmmmm," said the sewing machine man. He looked at the machine for a long time. "Tell you what," he said. "Why don't you trade this unit in on a new one and give your wife a real nice present?"

I nearly took his head off. I'm sure he meant well, but at the moment it just wasn't what I wanted to hear. When I calmed down, we talked rationally again. Something about a good cleaning and an alignment.

"Now we're talking," I said.

Back to the cell.

Finally, The Enemy and I began to see eye to eye. The machine was less belligerent, and I had decided to give it another chance. We had become friends, a team. We drilled those little stitches, 10-to-the-inch just like the instructions said. Make a seam. Stuff in the down. Make a seam. Stuff in the down.

I quit sweating. I quit swearing.

The booties began to look like the ones in the instructions. Finally, we stitched on those knit cuffs. Ta-dah!

It was still a few days before Christmas. Not since I was a kid had I waited with such anticipation for the day to arrive.

I was squirming when Phyllis began tearing the wrapping off the package. I relived the entire process as she stripped the paper off: the initial excitement, the frustration, the hate, the success.

She popped the lid off the box and stared at the booties. She loved them.

Never, before or since, has the giving of any gift thrilled me as much.

Every winter evening, Phyllis padded around the house in those things. Her feet were even warm when she got in bed at night. She wore them until they were tattered and battered, and she got another pair for a gift, fancy blue ones with padded soles and drawstring tops.

She still keeps the old orange ones in the corner of her closet. Both of us know why.

Find the Magic

We had been up before dawn, drinking tea and writing in our journals. Now it was almost sunset, and we had come perhaps 40 miles by dog-team and skis across the frozen sea that is Great Slave Lake.

The weather was good. It had been up to zero or maybe ten above during the day. We had skied ahead of the dogs without our wind parkas on.

Now, as the sun hung over the trees in the west, it seemed to be getting cold again. Our one-and-a-half-hour stints on the sled, behind the 11 dogs, were enough to make us want to ski again for the warmth it brought.

The dogs seemed fresh. Will Steger, whose dogs these were, also seemed fresh. He had donned his wind parka for this late afternoon shift on the skis, though he was wearing it unzipped in front. It flapped beneath his arms like some ungainly bird.

We were headed for a small Dogrib Indian village called Rae, about 100 miles by ice and dog team north of Yellowknife, Northwest Territories, on Great Slave. I had been with Steger only since Yellowknife.

My three-day sojurn with this dogged traveler from Ely,

Minnesota, was but a dash in the broken line that marked his journey on a map. The line began at Duluth, Minnesota. It would end at Point Barrow, Alaska. Five thousand miles. This hundred of it was like backing out of the driveway to go downtown.

"We'll have fun," Steger had said. "It'll be like winter camping."

We had done 12 or 15 miles the first afternoon, after a delayed getaway in Yellowknife. We had done 40 the next day, each of us skiing half the time ahead of the dogs. Now, we were that many miles again into the third day.

It would have been easy to stop and make camp. We could have cruised into Rae in full daylight the next morning.

But at sundown, Steger couldn't stop.

"I think we should go for it," he said. "I think it would be good for you to see what it's like to come into a village at night."

What we were going for was a point where the stunted spruce funneled together at the end of Great Slave's North Arm. We knew that's where the village of Rae lay.

The dogs liked the idea of going on. They could have gone all night at the same pace. Darkness enveloped us, and they seemed to perk up even more.

Over and over, the dogs and I caught up with the flapping form of Steger and would have to let him get out ahead again. The dogs would lunge and whine as his dark outline skied away and became one with the low horizon. Finally, I'd release the sled's snow hook and the dogs would trot steadily until it was time to repeat the routine.

I was tired. My legs were pieces of stale celery. My arms were limp pieces of spaghetti.

I was hungry. Our last meal had been breakfast—oatmeal in the tent. We had munched dried caribou during the day and drunk from our quart thermoses of water.

I guessed that Steger felt as I did. He is a tenacious traveler, but he is human. Yet, when we passed in the dark to exchange places on the sled and skis, he said nothing about his physical condition.

I put in another hour on the skis, searching the humps of crusted and wind-sculpted snow for the most passable route. Balance became a relative thing. I knew Steger and the dogs were behind me—catching up, waiting, moving again. But all I heard were the creaking of skis and chipping of my pole plants.

We changed places again and kept going into the night. The moon was up and nearly full. Then the northern lights appeared, a pale green arc across the northern sky. Wisps of green haze would shoot skyward from the arc, twisting and writhing, then recede again.

I was reminded of something another dog sledder, Lloyd Gilbertson of Finland, Minnesota, had said a few years before. "When the going's good, it's just magic."

That's what it was this night on Great Slave. The dogs, the moon, the movement, the northern lights—magic.

In the months since then I have had a lot of time to think about that evening. It is hard now to recall the fatigue I felt then, or to remember how much I'd have given for a bowl of beef stew.

It wasn't an easy day. But it was perhaps the most rewarding experience I had during a year that was not short on quality moments. The weariness had something to do with it, as much as the lights and the dogs and where we happened to be.

It has to do with immersion, I believe. Our lives are couched in comfort, cloistered with convenience. Rarely do we have the opportunity to immerse ourselves in an experience that lets us look inside our souls, to explore our boundaries, to flirt with the unknown. Even more rarely do we seize those opportunities when they are presented.

Sometimes, the opportunities occur when we least expect them. We don't plan them. We simply put ourselves in situations where such challenges are more likely to occur. It involves risking more than we might be accustomed to risking, biting off a little more than we are used to chewing.

It doesn't have to happen on Great Slave Lake. Or behind a dog team. Or in the heart of winter.

One of the most appealing things about living up north is that the opportunities to discover the awe of life abound. We have some big country out our back door. We have four stimulating seasons in which to encounter it. We have a wealth of people willing to take us there.

Go. Get out there. Feel the wind. Taste the rain. Find the magic.